Near' Straight Rows

Poetic Meanderings of
a Country Boy

Robert Johnston

Near' Straight Rows:
Poetic Meanderings of a Country Boy

Copyright © 2014 Robert Johnston

All rights reserved. No part of this publication may be reproduced, stored in a retrieval system or transmitted in any form by any means, electronic, mechanical, photocopy, recording or otherwise, without prior written permission of the author, except as provided by USA copyright law.

Scripture quotations are from The Holy Bible, English Standard Version ®, copyright © 2001 by Crossway Bibles, a publishing ministry of Good News Publishers. Used by permission. All rights reserved.

Cover Photo: Nate Brelsford
Image Credit: Valentine Heart Arrow Clip Art from Vector.me (by xunoe)

Printed in the United States of America

Printed by Createspace, an Amazon.com Company

ISBN-13: 978-1505365870
ISBN-10: 1505365872

To Peg and the children, Tim and Emily,
and the grandchildren, Harper Kay, Robert Henry,
Charles Carey, and Betsy Kate. And beyond...

*All the times we're near you,
you're being snuggled, hugged, and kissed.
Know that the times we are apart
are the times you're being missed.*

Contents

Introduction   8

Outdoor Poems

The Woods	10
Near' Straight Rows	12
Mr. Dragonfly	16
Treefall	18
Clouds	20
Love Birds	21
November's Rain	22
Two Old Dogs	24
Upstream	28
Storm Birds	30
River Dreams	32
Frequent Flyers	36
Wild Mountain Flowers	38

Family Poems

Family Ties	40
Mine	43
A Gentle Home	44
The Sunday Meal	46
Quality Time	48
Boonga Lives	50
The Cage	52
Sundays With Emily	57

My Grand Slam	60
Still Her Mom	62
Granddads	64
Near a Lake	66
Harper, Age Three	68
For Harper, Who Likes Lions	69
The Washtub Gang	70
Little Charlie	72
Two Bears	73
Betsy Kate	74
I Had It All	76
On Million A Year	78
Eulogy for Mom: "A Force of Nature"	81
Peace	84

Poems about "Me and Her"

For Peggy	86
Ever a Maiden	88
My Honeysuckle Rose	90
Angel	92
The Look	93
The Sad Days	94
The Ring	96
My Other Life	99
The Boy in the Mirror	102
Hold...	104

Lighter Poems

Underneath It All	106
Little Redneck Boys	108
Payday Thursday	110
A Monkey's Business	114

Old Lance	116
Sweet Women	118
Tank Commander Steve	120
Ode to Empty Nesters	122
No Deer	123
Sharpshooters	124
The Lazy Man	128
Dentally Challenged	130
Wackos and Liars	132
The Bathtub	133
Morning Banter	134
At the Zoo	135
Bank on It	138
The Chicken	140

Game Time Poems

The Game	145
The Stadium	146
My Buddy Joe	148
Our Team	150
Baseball Time	152
The Fighter	154
The Last Fourth Quarter	156

Poems in General

Tread Gently	158
Heroes	159
The Parting	162
The New Man	164
The Slow Lane	168
Accident of Birth	170
Classic Class Warfare	172

Unseen Hands	174
Vines	176
One Hundred Four and Counting	178
Questions	180
At the Indigo	181
Two Go In	182
Rooms of our Hearts	184
A Need for Speed	185
Federalies	188
For Noah	190
Tattooed	192
The Hound	194
Home	196
The Innocents Lost	198
Whisper	200
The Critical Man	201
Green	204
The Patch	206
In Appreciation	209

-§-
To be a poet is a condition, not a profession.
Robert Frost

Introduction

I have created poetry for as long as I can remember. Little poems to make people laugh. I would changed lines in songs from the radio and church hymns just for the fun of it.

I wrote poems in school just for grades or even for extra points in some English classes. Never once did I consider it seriously or even as a hobby. Until two years ago on one sleepless night, a phrase continually ran through my mind. I rose from the bed to drink some milk and grabbed a legal pad by my chair. Out poured my first poem, "Two Old Dogs." It is a pro-life poem that took three hours and a quart of milk to complete.

So why write a book of poetry now at this stage in my life? Honestly, because these things matter to me, and things that matter should be preserved and celebrated.

As a husband, father, and grandfather, passing a legacy to the next generations is of great importance. The love I have for my family, and that they have for me, is something worth celebrating. So is the dignity of human life, the enjoyment of God's creation, and the simple pleasures and humor that make up our lives. Publishing these poems is a part of that celebration.

Thank you for giving this book a chance.
I hope it makes you think and smile.
Grandkids, enjoy your childhood days,
and we'll be loving you all the while.

Robert Johnston
McCalla, AL
November 14, 2014

Outdoor Poems

The Woods

Now the woods are clean again,
washed by God's own rain.
Clean is the air, clean again,
free of the scent that tells of man.

A doe lifts her neck and tastes the air
to decide if there is danger near.
Yearlings and half year old fawns
watch her as they graze at dawn.

They can tell by her composure
if it is safe to graze from the woods to the pasture.
A young buck watches farther off today.
He was her fawn, but now mature,
she's driven him away.

He will be on his own now; he is mature.
He will hold his own now; he will endure.
He will mate and see his genes passed down.
He will wear his antlers like his crown.

He will run and chase and fight and mate
'til one day, too, he will meet his fate.
Be it canine's bite or hunter's round,
his blood will one day soak the ground.

The woods that once were fresh and clean
again will wear a scarlet stain.
The hawk will tear at his remains,
nature playing it's old refrain.

A doe lifts her neck and tastes the air
to see if there is danger near.
A young buck watches from far away.
He was once her fawn, but older now,
she has driven him away.

He is on his own now; he is mature.
He will hold his own now; he will endure.
He will mate and see his genes passed down.
He will use his antlers to defend his ground.

And in a plan set forth
by God's own grace,
a buck fawn will grow
to take his place.

12-6-13

Near' Straight Rows

We all knew why they came,
    the woman and the man.
Peace in their later years
    was what they had planned.

    Back to the land
        from whence they came,
    away from the back breaking
        rat race game.

Rest for their souls
    was what they had in mind,
something long ago
    which they had left behind.

    Their working lives over,
        they wanted to farm
    while there was still strength
        in their backs and their arms.

And the sun still set.
    And the moon still rose.
And the corn grew tall
    in near' straight rows.

The years flew by.
>	Seasons came and went.
Nearly twenty years
>	of their lives had been spent.

And the moon would still rise,
>	seen now with tired eyes –
one spring left to plant,
>	one summer left to watch the corn rise.

>	That winter, through all of
>	>	the storms and the cold,
>	God reached down to
>	>	the earth below

and plucked the man
>	from his bed of pain,
never to tend
>	his corn again.

>	Then He returned
>	>	in just a few years
>	to relieve the woman
>	>	of her doubt and fears,

lest she grow tired
>	of being alone
and her old heart
>	return to stone.

And the moon
> will rise
in the very
> same skies.

And the grass
> will now grow
where corn was planted
> in near' straight rows.

> The earth doesn't need
>> women and men
> to repeat this cycle
>> again and again.

The sun will rise;
> the sun will set.
It's been so forever;
> it's still so yet.

> God is the reason
>> men were born.
> We are here for his glory,
>> like our rows of corn.

And the moon still rises.
> And the grass still grows.
How long it continues,
> only God knows.

5-30-14

-§-
*The earth is the Lord's and the fullness thereof,
the world and those who dwell therein,
for he has founded it upon the seas
and established it upon the rivers.*
Psalm 24:1-2

Mr. Dragonfly

I've seen what you do.
You, sir, are a liar.
With your opaque wings
reflecting the sun's fire,

how often have you rested
on my fishing line
just like a tiny angel.
Who knew what was in your mind?

I saw you through my kitchen window
attack the Big Red Wasp.
You avoided the potent stinger.
Without that his cause was lost.

You attacked him head on,
directly face to face.
You began to shred him like a machine;
you ate him all, no waste.

You ate his head, his body,
his legs, and things.
And for dessert
you ate his wings.

The Big Red Wasp
will sting no more,
since you killed him
outside my kitchen door.

A question for you,
Mr. Dragonfly –
How can you eat so much,
then fly so high?

I tried to imagine
how I would feel,
trying to fly after
such a big meal.

One more question,
if you'll answer me,
have you ever eaten
a bumblebee?

4-24-14

Treefall

A tree fell
in my backyard,
sixty feet tall. When he hit,
he hit the ground hard.

He was a healthy oak,
a tall heavy-limbed tree.
He housed birds and squirrels,
and shaded folks like me.

After big rains and high winds,
the soft ground gave way.
He'll have to be cut up to use.
I have work to do today.

I've counted his rings.
We are about the same age,
over half a century, young for a tree,
half a century, near my ending stage.

I had pruned him last fall
and freed him from vines.
I thought to myself,
"He'll be here for some time."

Well, so much for
that wisdom of mine.
The wind blows where it will;
the rain falls in God's time.

I never thought myself to be much
of a tree hugger –
not one named Butterfly or Flutterby
or some rainbow dressed "bugger."

But I do admit,
I hate to see them fall.
They provide us with so much
while they ask for nothing at all.

8-29-14

-§-

*God said, "Let the earth sprout vegetation, plants yielding seed,
and fruit trees bearing fruit in which is their seed, each
according to its kind, on the earth." And it was so.*
Genesis 1:11

Clouds

The clouds above
        are just a mist.
For God's own pleasure,
        they do exist.

To see the sun
        when it's going down,
fiery orb throwing light
        from behind a cloud,

I often think it's
        the face of God, so bright,
dispeller of dark,
        Creator of light.

But then I know
        this can't be true.
Nobody's ever seen Him,
        neither I nor you.

But while Moses was shown
        only God's hinder parts,
we've been given His Spirit
        to live in our hearts.

8-7-14

Love Birds

A sad lady robin perched on a low limb.
> Her mate was below; she called softly to him.

But he couldn't answer, he was injured and weak.
> She landed beside him and nuzzled his beak.

She sat there with him all day and night.
> She was still around when the sun brought first light.

She awoke that morning with him under her wing.
> And though he had passed, she would still try to sing.

But all of this drama had not gone unseen.
> A young boy had watched it through his window screen.

He called in his dad and shared this with him –
> the robins below, in the grass, on the limb.

His dad said, "When birds mate, they do so for life.
> The birds you are seeing are husband and wife.

"They share a trait much more than emotion.
> What you have seen, son, is called devotion.

Humans once had it, now it's hard to find.
> It's now so rare, it can be hard to define.

It can be learned, and it may take a while,
> but to share it with someone makes it all worthwhile.

One day you'll find someone and set her apart.
> Nobody else will get a piece of your heart.

And if in return she feels that way for you,
> you'll find that devotion is love, when it's true."

There are things in this world to be learned from the birds.
> If you'll only observe, they say a lot without words.

And yet somehow, and it might be our sin,
> in this one way, birds may be better than men.

5-10-13

November's Rains

Most people stay inside on rainy days,
as if being damp is some kind of sin.
All of my life has been lived outside,
and I've been wet time and again.

Springtime rain can overwhelm
and can be pretty rough.
Especially if they bring strong winds
and lightning from the Gulf.

Summertime showers
can be a joy,
leaving rivulets and puddles
to be used by little boys.

Rain in the South
in early fall can be rare.
We look for clouds in the sky,
everyday, everywhere.

But it's the rains of November
I love to see arrive.
They can make a dreary day
seem to come alive.

They pour down hard and steady.
They help bring life to us all
by refilling lakes and rivers
left low by drought in the fall.

The best ones come
and pour straight down,
with no wind to blow
your umbrella around.

A November rain can
last all day
and fall at such
a steady rate

they'll wash dead leaves
from sleeping trees,
leaving just a few to fall
in December's freeze.

When next November
rolls around,
I'll listen for
that pouring sound,

pull on my boots
at the hunting camp,
and enjoy the woods
while they are damp.

Go out and wake the deer up
right where they sleep.
God sends in November rains,
memories for me to keep.

2-4-14

Two Old Dogs

Two old dogs lie in the sun,
feeling the warmth from up above.

The yellow one said to the old black lab,
"How come there are no kids around?
We need them to run and chase,
and lick the ice cream from their face.

"We need a boy to throw a ball,

> "So we can fetch
> it back, all wet,
> and he can pet
> us on our heads.
>
> "We need a girl
> with a comb and a brush,
> and she would take
> good care of us."

The old black lab said to the yellow one,
"There are no daughters here, no sons.
It was years ago when it was done.
I sensed that there would be a son

"when I saw the glow on the woman's face,
but her joy was all erased.
Her man was mad and all upset;
he said 'We don't need a baby yet.'

"So that young seed
was swept away.
And there is no boy
to help us play."

"But wouldn't they still
love a girl,
with sweet smiles,
brown eyes, and curls?"

"My yellow friend, I'm ashamed to say,
their little girl ended the very same way.
Pain was all they had to give;
she was not allowed to live –

"Not allowed to
play and grow,
or learn to love
her Mother so.

"Not allowed to live
and breathe,
to see the sun
or grass so green.

"And that's why we are all alone.
Our humans chose to end their own."
The yellow one said to the old black lab,
"Then that means we are all they have.

"And we know dogs don't live that long;
one day we'll leave them all alone."

Two old dogs lie by the road
and wait for the school bus to unload,
to share their love with a neighbor child,
who always stops to play for a while.

> But inside their
> human's home,
> the woman spends
> her time alone.
>
> And every day
> she'll turn to stare
> at the boy and the girl
> who were never there.

10-30-12

-§-
*Heaven goes by favor; if it went by merit,
you would stay out and your dog would go in.*
Mark Twain

-§-
For you formed my inward parts;
you knitted me together in my mother's womb.
I praise you, for I am fearfully and wonderfully made.
Wonderful are your works;
my soul knows it very well.

Psalm 139:13-14

Upstream

We traveled two thousand
miles to see them –
just part of the scenery
that fall season.

Salmon swimming
up a stream,
all dead set
on fulfilling their dream.

Their eggs are laid
and fertilized.
The salmon, now weak,
begin to die.

Every year it's
always the same.
They lay their eggs
so life can start again.

There are parts of humans
that share this dream.
Men have the swimmers.
Women have the stream.

A swimmer sets out
feeling incomplete,
not quite sure
what he is about to meet.

His other half
seems so far away,
upstream and ready
to be found today.

These are the wilder parts
of us, you see.
They unite to allow
our kind just to be.

These are
our wilder parts,
not always connected
to our heads and our hearts.

Though incomplete
they were both alive.
Together, a child like us
is formed to thrive.

So there's no question
when life begins.
It starts when woman
is joined by man –

as soon as the swimmer
makes his way upstream,
and finds his other half,
his dream.

10-29-13

Storm Birds

They know when it's coming,
    I was told as a child.
They know what to do;
        they know where to hide.

I was asking about birds
    when I was a boy.
A tornado was coming
        with high winds and noise.

Where would they go?
    Will they come back today?
What about their babies?
        Will they take them away?

I worried about them
    when I was a child.
I could see them in the pasture
        and on the telephone wire.

With a child's love and compassion,
    I considered them my friends.
Life was so simple
        for a young boy back then.

The robins and sparrows
    and those cocky old crows,
bright cardinals and loud blue jays
        put on quite a show.

Fifty years later
> another storm came our way.
This one took houses and barns
> and some old friends away.

As we helped some good people
> gather up what they owned,
I remembered my questions
> about birds, long ago.

I began to look – to see if
> any could be found
amid all the rubble
> strewn on the ground.

It didn't take long until
> the first birds were found.
They were battered and beaten
> and dead on the ground.

In answer to my questions,
> I now make my best guess.
Seems birds, before a storm, may
> fly home to their nest.

While we do the same,
> our homes make us feel safe,
but friends lost in a storm,
> unlike birds, can't be replaced.

4-14-14

River Dreams

The water was green.
There were lily pads.
I was having as much fun
as I'd ever had.

I was a young boy,
and I knew well how to fish.
A day at the river
was all I could wish.

There was a little girl
telling tales of "water babies and sprites."
I paid her no mind;
I was getting a bite.

I felt the fish on the line.
I felt him bend my cane pole…
But the alarm clock went off.
I was wounded to my soul.

A drive into town
put me back on the job.
I couldn't help feeling, somehow,
I'd been robbed.

To make matters worse,
it was a beautiful day,
the day you imagine
when you think about May.

The side of town where
I would work that day
was all mansions and gardens,
Old Money all the way.

Even the butlers and maids
all had frowns on their face –
such a beautiful day,
such a rich, arrogant place.

I drug myself around
and made my normal stops,
until I saw an old man,
wet with sweat from toes to top.

He was weeding flowers,
zinnias and roses on a bush.
He spoke and wiped his forehead,
the only man in Moneyville not in a rush.

He said, "You look a little down today."
I said, "I dreamed I was fishing at the river."
"Oh no," he said, "A dream about fishing this time
of year is the worst thing your mind can deliver.

"I've had those dreams from time to time,
and I hate it when it happens in May.
When I was about your age, it happened,
and I was no good for three or four days."

I thanked the man and went on with my job.
At least I knew I was not insane.
It had the same effect on this old man,
and it could happen to me again.

After talking to him, I realized
I'd had the worst kind of Fisherman's Luck –
to want to be fishing so bad you can taste it
on a day when you have to work.

4-16-14

-§-
*There is no greater fan of
fly-fishing than the worm.*
Patrick F. McManus

Frequent Flyers

Most people don't use them
here in the South.
They all use them up North
for rainbow trout.

    Most places down here, for trout,
    the water's too warm.
    You just go fishing for bass
    with a plastic worm.

People see me fish with it
and think it looks odd.
It's a fragile looking thing
called a fly rod.

    With a light weight line
    and a small yellow fly,
    you'll catch a boat load of bream
    before lunch time.

And with just a little luck,
fool a bass now and then;
but if he's over three pounds,
good luck reeling him in.

    A big bass will wreck your tackle
    and leave you empty handed.
    A heavy rod and tippet
    for him is recommended.

For bonefish in the Gulf,
steelhead in the Great Northwest,
for a lot of fishing fun,
a fly rod may be the best.

> You don't just bait your hook
> and wait for fish to smell or see,
> but to cast a bug or fly
> is a rare form of artistry –

to make it fall through the air
like a real bug oughta,
and land by the weeds
with just a ripple on the water.

> It takes a lot of practice
> to learn the proper motion.
> And for a fly fisherman
> it is a true devotion.

So no matter how you use it,
for steelhead, bream or bass,
the joy is not just in the catch,
but also in the perfect cast.

10-9-13

Wild Mountain Flowers

There's a Wild Mountain Flower in a row with the corn.
She had waited for the hour, for a chance to be born.
Somehow her seed had been planted here,
where there was not another flower near.

She had everything it takes to grow –
the mountain rain, the fertile ground below,
the sun each day to warm her mother, Earth.
But she had no one to understand her worth.

The plowman's blade dislodged her roots one day,
and like the trash, she was thrown away.
By human eyes her beauty was not seen.
She was in a place "she should not have been."

There's a Wild Mountain Flower awaiting to be born.
In this untimely hour, her Mother seems so forlorn.
She'd have everything it takes to grow,
and this young child would love her Mother so.

Someone needs to tell her mom the worth
of giving this young child her birth.
The doctor's knife is like the plowman's blade,
it will cut your Wild Mountain Flower away.

Make sure her beauty is truly seen by man.
You're her mom, the only one who can.
For your Wild Mountain Flower give thanks to the LORD.
Tell your Wild Mountain Flower you're so glad she was born.

9-19-13

Family Poems

Family Ties

I always thought I was
meant to be
in the woods and fields,
wild and free.

> Now, it's too late to be free
> of locks and gates
> and other things
> I grew to hate,

>> all things that make
>> a working man
>> buy his goods on credit,
>> on the "family plan."

It's my family ties
that kept me here,
things that some men
don't want to hear.

> Things like a loving wife,
> a daughter, and son,
> will cause you to work
> 'til daylight's gone.

>> To come home and see
>> my family's faces
>> restores all the colors
>> a hard day erases.

What I would have missed
in another life,
had I not known
my kids and wife!

    How dreary and dull
    would have been all
    without little league
    and girls volleyball.

        To see them now
        as young adults –
        I know their Mother's work
        brought good results.

They're good people
in spite of me.
Seems they didn't inherit
my stupid gene.

    But I'll brag some now,
    if you let me. You see,
    I picked my children's
    mom correctly.

        So what if I'm
        not free to roam,
        to fish and hunt each day
        'til the cows come home,

to live in a cabin
out in the woods
(short on many
store-bought goods),

    to eat squirrel and rabbit
    and bathe in a creek,
    to wear my blue jeans
    until they reek?

        For me God had
        a different plan.
        He meant for me
        to be a family man.

I know now, home
is where you find it,
if you put your
heart behind it.

    We never know
    where home will be,
    but I've bet my life
    she'll be with me.

        And I'll be with her
        until my life is done,
        because she warms my heart
        like the morning sun.

12-2-13

Mine...

Mine... mine can be so hard to define.
Is it a place to live that you can buy on time?
Can it really be yours if you don't have the deed
with your name on the line for the world to read?

We all need a place to go at the end of the day.
So if we call it mine, we say it's okay.
Of all the people you know, who do you claim?
Those in your family with the same last name?

I found that for me, that didn't always work –
even your kinfolks can behave like jerks.
I think someone did some pruning on my family tree
and lopped off all the branches that thought like me.

When I got married it worked out just fine.
I had all the legal papers to prove she was mine.
It took patience and love for us both to stay,
and all these years later, she's still mine today.

Our children came later. It was finally to be.
I put down my own roots to a new family tree.
They caused a new feeling in this heart of mine.
I learned what the word meant for the very first time.

Mine... really mine.

9-7-13

A Gentle Home

Homes should have more pictures
    than they have frames,
        and a story to go
            with every name.

There may be dust
    on every floor,
        but not one child
            would be ignored.

Kind words could
    still be found;
        love would grow
            in fertile ground.

Dad would never
    go away.
        He loves your mom
            enough to stay.

The Hand of God
    controls this place.
        They live day to day
            on His unchanging grace.

A gentler place
    can not be found.
        A family's love
            should know no bounds.

11-24-13

-§-
The homemaker has the ultimate career.
All other careers exist for one purpose only –
and that is to support the ultimate career.

CS Lewis

The Sunday Meal

It was a staple at our
home on Sundays,
long before our
kids moved away.

That aroma snaking slowly
up the stairwell
chased away your sleep,
and made you hungry as well.

Anointed with honey
like a prophet's head with oil,
it was sugar-cured and wrapped
with care in aluminum foil.

A ham in the oven meant
a family well fed.
A sermon that same morning,
for your soul, was the bread.

On most every Sunday
here in the South,
for most every family,
this scene was played out.

Or, if you were sick
or maybe away,
your TV had replays
of a Billy Graham Crusade.

Billy said God taught him
to "just preach the cross."
Bringing God's own Gospel to
the millions who were lost.

Some of us were poor
down here in the South,
but we were made rich
by the Gospel spread by mouth.

While I sit here reflecting
on what made us who we are,
I know our kids remember;
they won't have to think back too far.

We had that special meal on Sunday –
something good, like a ham,
and fed our souls on the Gospel,
preached by men like Billy Graham.

10-20-13

Quality Time

Quality time is what the experts
> preach to us these days.
And they can tell you how to spend it
> in so many ways.

What makes them so smart?
> I don't understand.
I've learned to take my quality time
> any way that I can.

Laughing with other workers
> while we sweated in the Alabama sun
helped to shorten a long, hard work day,
> and made working almost fun.

To help my own sweet wife
> get through a bout with the flu
is quality time for me,
> because she helps me when I'm sick too.

Spending time with my kids
> way back when they were small,
I chased so many baseballs,
> then "tea time" with my daughter
> 'til I drank it all.

An honest talk with God
    is always time well spent.
I confessed today, I don't know
    where the last thirty years went.

I worked so much back then
    quality time was hard to find.
Even though there was much less of it,
    it's the part that comes to mind.

Alone with myself, hunting today
    high up on the hill,
just me and God's creation
    is quality time, for me it's still a thrill.

1-14-14

-§-
Choose this day whom you will serve...
as for me and my house, we will serve the Lord.
Joshua 24:15

Boonga Lives

"Come inside, Tim,
there's not much daylight.
Put your toys by the tree
and tell Boonga goodnight."

> He lived in our garden
> for a very short time,
> a friend of my son,
> a vision of his mind.

Our garden was small
and surrounded by trees.
Our son played there for hours
with pail and shovel, and soil on his knees.

> He began to tell us
> of someone he knew.
> His name was Boonga,
> he was sure it was true.

We watched him as
he played alone
and heard him speak
to souls unknown.

> He seemed content
> in the garden out back
> with Boonga, his toys,
> and our big dog named Jack.

We asked about Boonga
every few days
to see if by chance
he had gone away.

> "Would Boonga like
> to come in and eat?"
> "No, Dad, he's under the
> bean vines already asleep."

Or, "Does Boonga need
to come in and bathe?"
"Mom, Boonga doesn't
have to wash his face."

> He was there for the summer,
> friend to our sweet child.
> Was he a vision from above
> or young imagination wild?

He's part of our family history.
A sweet memory for us to keep.
Boonga in our garden,
under our bean vines, fast asleep.

10-12-14

The Cage

Back when my son was
about ten years of age,
he asked me if we could
build a batting cage.

So I talked to my friend,
a high school coach up the street.
When I found out the price,
I just looked down at my feet.

But my friend said, "Don't worry
about buying that big old net.
All a boy needs
is a place to swing the bat."

So I went home to the yard
and surveyed the trees.
I said, "Son, we'll hang two lines
of fence right between these."

We had two lines of trees,
post oak and pine,
thoughtfully arranged
in two perfect lines.

When I showed my son
how the trees were arranged,
he said, "Dad, God must have
wanted me to have this cage!"

Tim used that cage,
and the neighbor kids too.
They all played ball
right through high school.

Through all the years,
it finally came,
the last time I'd pitch
to him before a game –

the High School All-Star Game
near downtown.
After this he'd play in college
and not be around.

Under a bluebird sky
and the shade of our trees,
I had worked up a sweat.
I said, "That's enough for me."

I was pleased with the way
he was swinging the bat.
I thought to myself,
"He needed that."

Retrieving the balls,
the bat, and the glove,
I heard words that
seem to have come from above.

"He didn't need that,
Robert, you did!"
All these years, I thought
this was just for my kid.

I didn't argue with God,
He's always right.
But I thought of the words
later that night.

"He didn't need that,
Robert, you did,"
were the words that continually
ran through my head.

Now I'm satisfied that
God, being God,
had a way to return me
to my boyhood backyard.

Again be the boy
who grew up and moved away,
while I pitched to my son
in the cage every day,

to bond with someone
like I didn't do then,
to have someone
for a lifelong friend,

to try and remember
what I had forgot,
to make the connections,
I had made not,

to forget the part of
my boyhood gone bad,
to cover and recover
from the words that were said.

But what was in store
for my son, Tim?
If this was for me,
then what was for him?

Did all the times that he spent
with the bat in his hands
even contribute to his
becoming a man?

Would he look back and ask,
"How much time did I spend,
when I could have been
hanging out with my friends?"

Well, one thing for sure,
he learned how to hit,
all his time in baseball –
he more than proved it.

And this one thing's for certain,
sure as the ball fits the glove,
as he travels through life,
my son will know he is loved.

10-12-13

-§-
To us, family means putting your arms around each other and being there.
Barbara Bush

Sundays with Emily

There have been times
> for me both good and bad.
I guess I was a child
> 'til I became a dad.

> I was a man at work,
>> a husband at home,
> but children taught me
>> what I had never known.

My son came first,
> a sight for my sore eyes.
Masculine was he; clenched fists
> appeared with his cries.

> Memories stirred from
>> deep in my soul,
> bringing back to mind
>> thoughts that had grown cold.

He was loud and strong,
> didn't like to be held.
He was the pride and joy
> of our little home as well.

"He is just like you were
    when you were that age,"
is what all my older
    relatives would say.

As he would grow,
    I loved being his dad.
He let me share in his childhood,
    for that I am glad.

Nearly three years later
    his sister was born.
She landed on earth
    the week of a great storm.

Gentle and quiet
    almost from the start,
it was plain to see,
    she was a lady at heart.

Saturdays were spent
    playing ball with my boy.
Sundays brought me a
    different kind of joy.

She owned me Sundays,
    because as a rule,
we took them to church
    and Sunday School.

She would sit on my lap
    during the sermon and sleep.
She never woke up at all,
    never made a peep.

My wife's Sunday meals
    were special for us all.
So while we waited, we looked
    at books or watched football.

    She was so easy to teach
        and eager to learn,
    though which one was the pupil,
        would be hard to discern.

What did I learn from my child?
    Sweetness, like you've never seen.
She must have drawn it from her mother,
    for there is none in my genes.

    That love can be pure
        and unconditional all the while,
    that kind of love comes only
        from a child.

8-4-14

My Grand Slam

Every hitter knows the feel,
if only one time,
      his dream comes real.

      The feel of the bat when it meets the ball,
      seeing it leave the yard before
            it starts to fall.

And if every base has a runner on,
the pitcher knows it's a grand slam
      he's just thrown.

      In my baseball life the grand slam escaped me.
      But I'll tell of another one,
            if you'll let me.

It was nothing that I did alone,
like swing a bat and watching the
      ball 'til it's gone.

      I was allowed a part in a greater plan,
      to be a father
            once again.

Her first cry was heard on a September day
while a hurricane was
      blowing our way,

      surely a gift from the Heavenly Father.
      And I still thank Him for her good looks,
           like her mother.

Full of grace in spirit and form,
she's been that way since the
      day she was born.

      Our friends called her "the perfect child,"
      but when picked on by her brother,
           she'd bite once in a while.

Surviving my duct taped diapers
and her older brother,
      by God's grace, she took after her mother.

      Now she is a mother with babes of her own.
      I hope I'll be here to see them
           when they're big and grown.

When life's ballgame is over,
the Great Scorekeeper will say,
      this quite ordinary player
      hit a grand slam that September day.

3-6-14

Still Her Mom

*Written for a dear friend on the
occasion of her daughter's wedding*

So you're losing a daughter,
but gaining a son.
The *two* are no more,
they have become *one*.

    It happened to us
    not so long ago.
    It's the normal way things
    happen, you know.

There will be things to look for
in your future life.
You'll still be her mom,
even though she's his wife.

    She'll call you at home
    when her work day goes bad,
    and if she can't find you,
    she'll talk to her dad.

When life gets her down
'til she clenches her fists,
she'll need to see Mom,
you're first on her list.

When it's time to be
a mother herself,
your mothering skills
will come off the shelf.

She'll want you there with her
for a week or two,
to show her how and what
a mother should do.

You'll do all the work
while your little girl's resting,
then you'll go back home
and thank God for this blessing.

Anyway, that's how it's been
for us since the day
I walked down the aisle
and gave our sweet girl away.

We know you wish for her
the moon and stars,
because you love your daughter
the same way we love ours.

8-9-13

Granddads

I must have missed him
all of my life.
Now that I can look back
through years of hard work and strife.

Never thought much about him;
just somebody else I never had.
Still would have been nice, though,
to have had an old Granddad.

I did adopt a few along the way,
some older black men that I knew.
They took time to help this restless soul;
they showed me how to muddle through.

"Doc," Earnest, and "Schoolboy"
shared their wisdom and tales with me.
Just a lonely white face in a friendless place,
they taught me to be what I had to be.

It must be nice
for a boy who's small
to have someone
to help him play ball,

or read him a book
on a hot summer day,
or teach him a poem,
a few lines he can say.

But my childhood's long over,
my children are grown.
By God's grace I now have
grandkids of my own.

As long as I'm here,
their granddad will exist.
I'll try hard to give them
the man that I missed.

8-7-14

-§-
*I don't know who my grandfather was;
I am much more concerned to know
what his grandson will be.*
Abraham Lincoln

Near a Lake

Not far from a lake there is a home
underneath the mountainside.
This is the place we find our rest
from life's spectacular ride.

We watch deer from here,
fox and turkey too.
We love to hear the cry of the hawks
when they come screaming through.

February, we took the grandkids out
to play in the snow on the ground.
I glanced up at the sky and the mountainside
and from the mountaintop, soaring down,

a bald eagle was seen with widespread wings
in the bluebird colored sky.
We watched him sail; his white head and tail
were much to our delight.

He rode high on the thermals
produced by a gentle southern wind.
Sunlight through his feathers shown.
I hope I'm allowed to see him again.

We are blessed to be
at our home near the lake beneath the mountainside,
where we see Canada geese, hawks, and bald eagles
take their life's spectacular rides.

2-18-14

Harper, Age Three

She was here this week
for four or five days.

    A child who owns me
        in so many ways.
    She gladdens my heart
        and brightens my days.

With a smile so sweet,
    or sometimes a frown,
she easily tears
    my defenses down.

    She's so like her mother,
        our own little girl,
    who, along with her brother,
        changed my view of the world.

But she's her own person,
    make no mistake.
She'll be able to give
    much more than she takes.

    One day when she reads this,
        I hope she'll see
    how much we love Harper,
        her grandmother and me.

1-10-13

For Harper, Who Likes Lions

When we're all in Heaven
    one thing you can name,
and have just for fun, is
    a lion with a mane.

I know that down here
    lions may give a scare,
but we'll be in Heaven,
    there's no biting up there.

We'd wash him and brush
    him and comb out his mane.
I know to most people
    it would look insane.

A big rowdy pet for
    a man of my age?
But there's no need in Heaven
    for him to live in a cage.

We'd thank you, Lord Jesus,
    when we'd had our talk,
and ask you one day
    if we could fly like a hawk.

5-26-13

The Washtub Gang

Wanted: Freshly Diapered

I'm viewing a poster
of a brand new gang.
The only two members
are Charlie and Hank.

Charlie is on the right
with a big wide grin.
But be careful folks,
don't be taken in.

You can't tell it,
but this guy's a thief.
He'll steal your heart
and cause you all kinds of grief!

A master of disguise,
he can disappear in a fog.
He's wanted for biting
poor Lucy, the dog.

The one on the left
is known by his alias, "Hank."
He is already worth more
than all the money in the bank.

If you see him, folks,
it's best just to run!
He'll do you in with a grin.
He won't need a gun.

Now that you know
of his obvious charms,
please note: His crime is
sleeping only in his Daddy's arms.

If you catch them and hold them,
there is a big reward.
Your heart will be filled,
and your soul will be warmed.

So please be alert
and, whatever you do,
catch the "Washtub Gang"
before they turn two.

12-28-13

Little Charlie

Lying back on his bed,
>head resting on his hands,
>>grandson Charlie sleeps
>>like a little old man.

He earns his rest
>by the way he plays.
>>Never still, he grows a little
>>along the way.

He walks for miles
>and never leaves the room,
>>with the brightest smiles,
>>chasing away the gloom.

Like the other kids,
>he's our pride and joy.
>>And big sister truly loves
>>this little boy.

So play hard, Charlie,
>and dream so deep.
>>The angels watch over you
>>while you sleep.

3-12-14

Two Bears

We go up the stairs like two brown bears,
me crawling on achy knees.
My grandson, Henry, showing the way,
crawling here beneath me.

It's so much like when his dad
was small at our home.
We two brown bears on the loose,
on our knees we would roam

across the carpet
and up the stairs,
sniffing around, seeing what could be found,
like two nosy brown bears.

3-1-14

Betsy Kate

According to some
she did arrive late.
Maybe she'll keep her own time,
our new Betsy Kate.

    Then there were some
    who said "No, it's too soon,"
    of this sweet girl,
    born just before noon.

Whether late in our lives
or a little early in her term,
I feel certain there will be
plenty to learn

    from this beautiful child
    now just two days old,
    as we watch God's plan
    for her start to unfold.

She's fair of face
and long of limb.
Will she look like her dad,
my own son, Tim?

Or be dark of eye and hair
on a shorter frame?
Will she look like
his wife, her mother, Jaime?

Either way it's in the
hand of God, of course.
Another blessing from Him
has sprung forth.

A daughter for them,
grandchild for my wife and me,
and not to forget, playmate
for big brother, Henry.

9-11-14

-§-

*Behold, children are a heritage from the Lord,
the fruit of the womb a reward. Like arrows in the
hand of a warrior are the children of one's youth.
Blessed is the man who fills his quiver with them!*

Psalm 127:3-5

I Had It All

To have it all
has been the phrase
that answers every
question raised

about your life's aims,
your life's intent,
or how your time on
Earth will be spent,

or what you wish to gain
and what you'll do
with what you've earned
and what's given you.

I'm sure I've used that phrase
at least once or twice,
as a young man looking forward
to my future life,

for self motivation or a
true life goal,
not knowing that "things"
can take your heart, mind, and soul.

Now, looking backward,
I can see clearly:
Hindsight is not
nearly so bleary.

Material things once
thought to be treasure,
I know now were only
temporary measures.

I have come to know
by my own labor
what to let go
and what to savor –

a smile from my wife
or touch of her hand,
a grandchild's laughter
warms me time and again.

An old dog's yawn
on a hot summer day
can bring a smile to my face
in a "me too" kind of way.

Knowing our children
love God and work hard
is worth more than a mansion
with a finely trimmed yard.

Knowing, with these things,
I have been truly blessed.
If called Home right now,
my soul would surely rest.

My blessings from God
have been many, large and small,
and as I look back on them, I can truly say
I had it all.

5-9-14

One Million A Year

In years long ago when
    we were growing our boy,
the fact that he was here
    was enough to enjoy.

    Then came our daughter,
        our beautiful girl,
who added her light
    to our part of the world.

When they became older,
    it all became clear,
we would have to speak
    of the one million a year.

    But how do you speak gently
        of what's being done,
when men can dispose
    of their daughters and sons?

There's no other way,
    but to lay it out plain,
even if it may go
    against another man's grain.

And so it was,
>　and so it went.
Words like bullets
>　at a target were sent.

One million children, due
>　in the year you came along,
were each "confiscated."
>　Now they're all dead and gone.

>　Those kids today,
>　>　who would now be your age,
>　were all "disallowed"
>　>　at their earliest stage.

Your playmates and friends,
>　who today should be here,
have all "disappeared"
>　by one million a year.

>　They are not here –
>　>　one million a year.
>　Do you think there were some
>　>　that you might have held dear?

They are not here –
>one million a year.
Could there be even one
>that you may still want near?

>I hope that I've not
>>been too rough.
>But when will we
>>have had enough?

When will we all
>take a look around
and find ourselves
>on common ground,

>be men enough to
>>end the slaughter
>of our country's
>>sons and daughters,

be brave enough to
>save this portion
killed each year
>by legal abortion?

5-14-13

Eulogy for Mom: "A Force of Nature"

If you knew my mom
for very long,
you knew a woman
exceedingly strong,

tougher and smarter
than the norm,
with energy and strength
to rival a storm.

A force of nature
has met it's ebb,
not a storm that wove
a path of fear and dread.

A path of destruction
was not this storm's fame,
but one of will and strength
will be her claim.

A depression's child
from the old poor South.
A house with eleven kids worked
sun to sun for food in their mouths.

Their early breakfast
of thin gravy and biscuit bread,
while not a lot, filled the empty spot
and kept them fed.

Then her mom, she told me,
many times before,
fed the black neighbor children
out of her kitchen door.

She said they were just biscuits
made with lard,
but our grandma wouldn't let
those children starve.

It was from acts like these,
she learned her ways.
She was generous to a fault
'til her dying days.

From West Alabama,
with its hollows and hills,
to the Mississippi Delta,
with its cotton fields,

she tracked north
for a time to Illinois,
but settled near Birmingham
with its steel mills and noise.

When she was young,
she adopted a son;
a few years later,
a second one.

While our time at home
was usually merry,
those spankings
are still legendary.

I've joked with her
about them for a lot of years,
though sometimes, I took the licks
while she shed the tears.

An iron hand
in a worn cotton glove,
she disciplined strongly
to show me her love.

And since hard rain in a storm
falls down in torrents,
my pet name for her was
Hurricane Florence.

For ninety-one years
this storm has raged.
She's gathered strength and wisdom
as she aged.

She taught us a lot
while on this earth.
No one I know
ever questioned her worth.

While her thunder and lightning and winds
have calmed down,
she's still unbeaten, unbroken,
and only to God has she bowed.

2-9-14

Peace

The old folks have gone on now,
their failing bodies ache no more.
The grandchildren are playing,
with one more waiting to be born.

My wife is still lovely,
a sweet sight for my eyes.
God's spirit is among us
as He reigns from on high.

3-25-14

Poems about "Me and Her"

For Peggy

When I think back to my early teens,
to see your face was a thrill to me.
With your pretty eyes and shining hair,
you hardly knew I was even there.

Then came the fall and the football games,
you learned my face and then learned my name.
You were on the sidelines every time,
shaking your pom-poms, yelling your rhymes.

But I had to take two trophies home
before you spoke to just me alone.
And from that day a whole year went past,
'til you sat near me in English class.

I asked you out at the end of the year,
you told me, "I am busy, dear."
Later that summer, we were dating;
come September, you kept me waiting.

An old boyfriend was the first in line,
when I dialed your telephone that time.
Friday night after that football game
was the last night I spent out with the team.

We were on and off, but ever since,
those times with you are the best I've spent.
Since I took you from your Mom and Dad,
you've been the best friend I ever had.

It's been forty short years from that June
when we took our two-day honeymoon.
And as I sit here all lost in thought,
I know I chased you 'til I was caught.

Now I'm older, hopefully wiser.
There are some things that I have surmised, dear.
And if I'm asked for advice to give
about a young man's life to live,

It's – if you love and cherish your own wife,
you will love and cherish your own life.
It's not how much love you get, I've learned,
but the more you give, the more's returned.

If asked to speak on these forty years,
I'd just look at you and say thank you, dear.

6-12-13

Ever a Maiden

Was ever a maiden
so beautifully dressed
as the one I took out
in her green summer dress?

It was when we went out
for the second time –
a summer dress,
the color of lime.

I knew I was going to love her.

Did ever a maiden instill
in a mind such a mess,
as when she wore
that same green summer dress

with another boy
to watch me play?
From the football field I could see
her dress fifty yards away.

And I was the one who loved her.

Was ever a garment
so pleasantly hung
from shoulders of one
so tender and young?

A coat of fur,
warm and white,
I gave it to her
one Christmas Eve night.

Because I am the one who loved her.

Did ever a man
have a smile so bright
as when she accepted
my ring one night?

She took my ring;
she owned my heart.
And as I knew
right from the start,

I am still the one who loves her.

3-3-14

My Honeysuckle Rose

At a table in the mall,
  I tried to put some words on paper.
My wife kissed my cheek, went to shop,
  and said she'd be back later.

    As she turned to go,
      I touched her on her hand,
    went back to my work,
      and heard a question from a young man.

        "How long have you two been married?"
          the young man asked of me.
        I told him we were married
          in June of seventy-three.

He said, "That's a long time, sir.
  But when you asked for her hand,
how did you know you loved her enough
  for your marriage to stand?"

    I said, "I asked myself three questions.
      Number one, is she my princess?
    Yes, I thought, she's in my very head
      and leaves my mind in a mess.

        "Question two I asked myself
          was just a little bit hard.
        If she were my 'Lady Godiva'
          would I let her 'bareback' out in the yard?

"Yes, if the neighbors were blind
   and there was a really dense fog.
But if anyone tried to peek,
   I'd beat him like an old dog.

     "Question three was harder to me still,
       because I grew up in the South,
    where the scent of the rose is as sweet
       as honeysuckle in the mouth.

       "The taste of honeysuckle
         and the scent of the rose
      goes past the palate,
         and way down into the soul.

"They're embedded deep
   in every cell.
You may travel far and wide,
   but you'll retain their taste and smell.

     "So you see, young man,
       it was easy for me to know,
    for I had asked myself: Is she
       my Honeysuckle-Rose?

       "She's still my taste of honeysuckle
         and my sweet smell of rose,
      and I'll spend the remainder of my life
        with my Honeysuckle-Rose."

5-11-14
Mother's Day

Angel

I've heard there's an angel for everyone's life,
and I've had one angel and she's my wife.
My angel is good and kind and sweet
and the prettiest one I could hope to meet.

When I'm ready to let go and explode like a bomb,
my angel is there to help me stay calm.
She'll plead with her eyes, tug at my sleeve.
To keep me from a fight,
she'll say, "It's time for us to leave."

Those who knew us both from way back when
said, "Nothing can last between the two of them."
That just goes to show how wrong friends can be,
because my angel was put here on earth just for me.

The two of us still here,
held by one emotion.
No one but her has shown
me such devotion.

1-21-14

The Look

One of the greatest pleasure of my life
has been observing my own sweet wife.
She seldom knows that I'm even aware
of what she's doing when she's busy around here.

To see her cook has been a joy of mine.
If it's cake, I'll steal some batter every time.
I know you think that might be a waste,
but raw cake batter has a delicious taste.

She has her own way of doing things.
I've known that since she was seventeen.
Her expressions could fill a picture book;
for different things, she wears a different look.

But my favorite look from her all the while
is the look she wears when she holds a child,
from her teenage years as a babysitter,
to our own son and his baby sister.

It is a look devoid of all aggression,
a perfectly joyful love expression.
She can take the loudest howler crying,
and in a minute, he is cooing and sighing.

She still has The Look with our own grandkids.
It looks as beautiful now as it ever did.
This expression of hers is priceless to me,
and even now, it's a joy to see.

10-6-13

The Sad Days

I don't know where
>   you go sometimes.
You are here in your body,
>   but not in your mind.

I miss you so much
>   when you are like this.
I can see it coming,
>   and I know something's amiss.

I know that your life
>   has suffered great loss,
and living on earth will exact
>   a great cost.

A family like yours
>   was ever so rare,
to be without them for so long
>   will never seem fair.

You were so close to those
>   who've left you behind,
while I had never loved that deep
>   in my heart or my mind.

You see, in this respect,
    I have an advantage over you.
There was no one in my life
    to be that close to.

Now I'll remind you
    of the things you have done.
You carried and raised
    both my daughter and son.

You taught me about love and
    I guess how to act.
You've been my family, for real,
    as a matter of fact.

So when your "sad days" come around
    and your sweet smile has to leave,
I'll be here beside you,
    missing you, you can believe.

Or, you can take me with you
    the next time, when you go.
I'll be glad to tag along
    just because I love you so.

7-16-14

The Ring

I would never wear jewelry.
    Maybe I never found my style.
A puka shell necklace or a surfer cross
        seemed to be in my way all the while.

    I had a ring once,
        my senior high school year.
    I let my girlfriend wear it,
            she seemed to hold it so dear.

When I married the girl,
    we exchanged rings.
I thought to myself,
        "What will I do with this thing?"

    It pinched my hand
        when I wore it to work,
    but not wearing it
           made me feel like a jerk.

While cleaning my hands
    after working late,
I left it on my
        work truck's tailgate.

I thought about it
> while in a traffic jam.
I made a u-turn and
> went back to Birmingham.

That made me miss
> my night school class,
but my ring was safe
> when I got home, at last.

Another time, while driving
> a large trencher,
I had another
> ring misadventure.

The trencher, on a hill,
> started to flip and wreck.
I would have to jump off
> to save my neck.

Before I could rise
> and get to my feet,
my wedding ring hung
> on the metal seat.

I told my wife that night
        about what went on.
She said, "Just leave that
        ring of yours at home."

        But after all these years
                of holding her hand,
        it seems the wedding ring
                has become a part of this man.

It brings us closer
        when we're apart.
I just have to touch it to
        warm my heart.

        I think of her when
                I see its golden shine,
        while I can see her face
                in my mind's eye.

Like me, its dull at times,
        a little bent and old,
but it has its place, there with her,
        in my heart and in my soul.

6-27-14

My Other Life

I had another life
before you came,
before I had ever
heard your name,

> so long ago when
> I was a child,
> no one there like you,
> so sweet and mild.

No one spoke gently
at all back then.
I remember well,
the pain from their hands.

> No one to listen
> to what I had to say.
> I began to shut them
> all away.

To be with them
was to be in a fight,
anytime of the
day or night.

I found a way that
I could escape
when I had had
all that I could take.

I'd lock myself up
in my room
to escape all of their
doom and gloom.

I only came out
at times to eat.
Not seeing them
meant life was sweet.

Inside my room
were four bare walls.
I hung a map of the world
on the door to the hall.

No stereo, no phone,
no lamp, or TV,
just my bat, my glove,
football jerseys, and cleats.

A radio would be my company.
I played it sometimes in the dark.
I won it one Halloween in a game
throwing darts.

In that room I could
be somewhat self-contained
while I did my homework,
improving my brain.

It must have been
too much for them to take,
so they took my only
comfort away.

       In their quest
       to impose on me even more,
       they put my bed in a room
       with no closable doors.

So it was "on again"
'til I left home.
What I found in you,
I had never known.

       So dear, if sometimes
       I may snap at you or even bark,
       or my reply to you
       should feel too sharp,

remember, if you will,
from where I came,
and the life I had
before I learned your name.

       It won't be you
       I'm talking to,
       but the life I had
       before I had you.

6-9-14

The Boy in the Mirror

"Oh Woman Dear, what have ya done
  to the man in the mirror who looked like my son?

I look into his eyes, once bright and green.
  Now there's red in the corners and in between.

I see the teeth, once strong and white,
  who now threaten to crumble with every bite.

And his hair once brown and red and long
  is turning to white, and soon could be gone."

"It was not me," the woman replied,
  "The boy who was in your mirror has died.

He left one morning when the sky was red
  to do his job, to keep us fed.

He spent forty years in the sun and the rain.
    It was time, not me, who brought you this pain.

Now I tell you this, as true as I can,
    the boy may be gone, but in his place is the man."

"But," he asked while rubbing his chin,
    "Do you still love the man like the boy back then?"

"Now listen, old man, while I tell you the truth.
    I love the old man much more than the youth.

The anger that was once in your face
    is all but gone. It's been replaced

by a gentle look that shows me, dear,
    how much you care and still want me near."

The old man looked up to the moon above
    and was glad she saw him in the light of love.

8-1-13

Hold...

Hold my heart gently,
if you can.
By now it is in pieces,
and I'm just a man.

I'm not the rock I once was,
not the one you knew.
I let you come in,
now I depend on you.

Hold my heart firmly,
if you can.
It's been known to run
like water through your hand.

There are no more places
for it to try to hide.
So keep it next to yours,
hidden deep inside.

Hold my heart dearly,
don't let it beat alone.
I have come to learn, too late,
I was better made of stone.

5-16-14

Lighter Poems

Underneath It All

It's been a woman's plan
to control her own man
    strictly for torture, of course.
        A tool to guide and provide
          divine help from our brides,
like a bit in the mouth of a horse.

You may ask with disdain,
who could legally frame
    torture for men everywhere.
        My answer is short,
          more specifically, *shorts* –
the girl who first made underwear.

Is it so cold in July
that we can't go outside
    without an extra wrap on our rear?
        But it's the rule we abide,
          male bees can't leave the hive
without wearing our "good underwear."

If we all dared to fight
and went shortless tonight,
    would anyone know or care?
        Or would our towels and sheets
        take to the streets
    to save tighty-whiteys everywhere?

Thus, they affirm their beliefs
in boxers and briefs
    and torture for man's derriere.
        So when the worry and grief
        brought on by boxers and briefs,
    in the hot summertime, chafes the rear –

Just leave them at home,
they'll be okay alone,
    I promise they won't feel let down.
        But make sure your pants fit,
        they'll be no room for a split,
    when you're bare underneath, downtown.

9-6-13

Little Redneck Boys

Boredom arrives in Alabama
on any hot summer day.
Little redneck boys look for ways
to keep Old Man Boredom away.

Here's some stuff we learned
while growing up, and old, and obtaining grace.
I thank the Good Lord I'm still here
with two eyes and all of my face.

We did stuff like this
to prove and disprove old legends and myths,
but it sure kept us "skint" up
and walking around with temporary limps.

A jump off the roof
can be survived.
I'm here today as living proof
that, if you land on cardboard,
you will surely stay alive.

If you chop a snake into three pieces
all three of them will live.
Don't try it with an old cottonmouth moccasin,
the best advice I can give.

A Jersey milk cow will give you a ride.
They're mean as any brahma bull born.
Nevermind their udders and soft eyes,
  just take a look at those horns.

When you target practice with a BB gun,
hold the garbage can lid in front of your face.
You can dig a BB from a fat boy's navel,
  but his eye you cannot replace.

When your jousting like knights
  while riding your bikes,
and using two by fours for your lance,
make sure you get the longest one
or wind up on the seat of your pants.

When you play football long after dark
on an unlit playground with monkey bars,
remember where the monkey bars stand,
or loose your teeth and see some stars.

He may throw like a girl, the kid next door,
  but don't tease him to much for it.
Billy had a once-in-a-lifetime accurate throw,
  and mine was the head that caught it.

It may seem odd now, us growing up
  and doing these things as kids.
Just remember how often a redneck's last words
  are, "Hey, y'all, watch me do this!"

1-18-14

Payday Thursday

It was payday Thursday
one dark, cold November.
My birthday had just passed.
I was feeling old, I remember.

    Pay for two weeks hard work
    in the cold and the rain,
    for hard dangerous labor,
    my own fatigue and pain.

When I arrived at the bank,
there was an extra long line,
and leave it to me
to be the last one this time.

    When I got to the teller window,
    much to my surprise
    was a beautiful young girl
    with brilliant blue eyes.

Since I'd used this bank
for many years,
this young girl, I thought,
must be new working here.

What she did then
was to set the stage.
She said I looked so good
for a man of my age.

That statement right there
set off an alarm.
I ain't that pretty,
not in any shape or form.

As she counted out my bills,
she kept up a constant chatter,
the hundred dollar bills
and the smaller ones that matter.

I watched her hands as she counted
and ignored her big blue eyes.
I knew her flirtation
was a steady stream of lies.

She was all set to distract me
and make my money her own.
As hard as I had worked to earn it,
my money was mine, and mine alone.

When she finished counting
and flashing those blue eyes,
I said, "Darling, would you mind
counting my money one more time?"

> She just said okay
> and drew a deeper breath.
> I bet you can figure out
> just what happened next.

When she totaled up this time,
I was short a one hundred dollar bill.
She apologized, but all the while
the smile never left her lips.

> I told my wife when I got home
> what the young girl tried to do.
> My wife just frowned and said aloud,
> "Let that be a lesson to you.

"All young girls you meet out on the street,
especially ones half your age,
they all act so sweet,
but play a role, like they're up on the stage.

> "Men with untrained eyes
> can believe lies time and time again.
> And all their hard earned money
> will go on down that old proverbial drain.

"The bottom line is," she said to me,
"If they lie, you know they'll cheat.
From here on in, just to be safe, Dear,
bring your paycheck home to me."

1-8-14

-§-
The monkeys stand for honesty
Giraffes are insincere
And the elephants are kindly, but they're dumb
Orangutans are skeptical
Of changes in their cages
And the zookeeper is very fond of rum
Paul Simon

A Monkey's Business

There was a monkey hanging
high up in a tree,
calling to me loudly,
and throwing banana peels at me.

> He said, "Hey, old man,
> ain't you ashamed?
> Having it so easy,
> 'cause God gave you a giant brain?

>> "Of all the gifts God gives us,
>> the best must be a brain,
>> 'cause man is the only one I know
>> who sleeps inside, out of the rain."

"Now, hold on, Brother Monkey," I said,
"That's the first I've heard you talk.
You don't have it so bad, swinging through
the trees while I have to walk.

> "You live high in the trees;
> you are cooled by God's own breeze;
> you've got other monkeys
> to get rid of your fleas.

>> "You eat free bananas,
>> free mangoes and nuts.
>> And the world thinks you are
>> the cutest little mutts.

"We get nothing for free
in man's world, it's a fact.
And nearly half of what we earn,
we have to give back for tax."

> The monkey asked, "So what is this tax?
> I don't understand...
> Does someone take half of your bananas,
> just because you're a man?

>> "If a monkey comes to my house
>> to take half my bananas away,
>> I'd slap him off my tree limb
>> and say, 'Monkey, it don't work that way!'

"So pardon me for speaking, old man,
I see my mistake is plain.
I thought you were the smart one here,
but it seems I have the bigger brain."

> I continued through the jungle
> and thought *that little monkey's right.*
> I ought to move out here with them
> and sleep on tree limbs every night.

>> Then I hung my head sadly.
>> It would never work for me.
>> God made the monkeys different,
>> I wasn't built for climbing trees.

1-7-14

Old Lance

Here he sits, his rifle in his hand,
Old Lance Thomas, still hunting his land.
>   No other place
>   can show him such rest,
>   Lance in his boots,
>   with his gun and his vest,

in his shooting house on a power line,
now covered with briars and honeysuckle vines.
>   Nothing in the world
>   can scare him away.
>   He is in his best spot
>   and intends to stay.

He came here to hunt, and hunt he did,
with all the excitement of a little kid.
>   Some say Old Lance went
>   and stayed too long.
>   In the end, he
>   never made it home.

We went down to find him, and on our journey south,
I remembered his wish, spoken by his own mouth.
>   So we stopped and gathered
>   stone and cement.
>   I told the others,
>   "I think I know where he went."

At his shooting house on the power line,
where he'd spent so much of his time,
    his Browning was still
    raised to his shoulder.
    But Old Lance
    was slumped way over.

It looked like he had just taken a shot,
so I followed my eyes down to the food plot.
    There I saw the
    biggest buck I had ever seen.
    One shot at the shoulder
    had killed him clean.

A heart attack must have killed Old Lance.
But he pulled the trigger when he had his chance.
    So we sealed him up
    in his shooting house,
    to fulfill the wish he wished
    with his own mouth.

With rocks and mortar we sealed him in.
He'll be in his chair 'til Jesus comes again.
    But I left a small window
    to view his food plot,
    in case the Good Lord gives him
    just one more shot.

9-18-14

Sweet Women

When I begin to count all
the women in my life,
all these ladies rank right
up there alongside my wife.

Aunt Jemima caught my eye early.
She was my first true love.
Her pancakes were so light, it's
as if they came from heaven above.

Cover them with Golden Eagle Syrup,
include a side of country ham,
you'll see why the syrup jar says,
"It's the Pride of Alabam."

Next came Betty Crocker,
when I was just a boy.
Her yellow, white, and chocolate cakes
brought me a lot of joy.

I saw her picture on the box,
and though she did look sweet,
having to mix and bake the cake
proved to be too much work for me.

I moved on to look for easier prey, to
fulfill my basic need.
Dolly Madison came on strong,
but this "Ding-Dong" was just a "Ho-Ho."
I was afraid of where it might lead!

Sarah Lee. Just say her name,
how sweet it sounds to me.
But everyone's in love with her.
"Nobody doesn't like Sarah Lee."

Now I'm older, and I'm fully aware
that this might be a sin.
But my taste buds and my sweet tooth
have fallen in love again.

A younger woman attracts me now,
and she can really cook.
She turns my head at the Zippy-Mart, or
the hardware store. She's everywhere you look!

Little Debbie, can you have mercy on me?
Your creme pies are keeping me fat.
We have to break up, you know it's true,
it's as simple as that.

No more of your Fudge Rounds
at night, when it is late,
and please keep your Zebra Cakes
away from my plate.

It must be this way,
Little Debbie. You see,
you're much too sweet
for a fat boy like me!

9-17-14

Tank Commander Steve

Tank Commander Steve
is ready to go.
His big machine is set to roll.
Commander Steve is in battle mode.

There is none better
in the world.
He enlisted young
to impress the girls.

He leads his men
through a subdivision.
The natives sneer and pinch
their noses with derision.

He spots his troops
already digging in.
He knows in his heart
it's time to begin,

as he swings his deadly tube around,
to aim it at a hole.
Here Commander Steve takes
his deadly toll.

Commander Steve doesn't kill Afghans
or shell Iraqis.
He destroys "Poop Monkeys"
and piles of "Hockey."

A Hero he is.
He is the one to thank.
He is the best at
cleaning your septic tank.

So the next time
your nose feels insulted –
an overflow
may have resulted

when your overfed, old
fat friend, Robert,
who ate until his
big tummy hurt,

tried to flush
it all away,
down the pipe
the very same day.

Don't let your yard
carry the stain
of a septic tank
that refuses to drain.

Tank Commander Steve
is the name to call.
He loves your tank;
he commands them all.

11-22-13

Ode to Empty Nesters

Your time is now here.
It's what you've waited for.
Your youngest child
is out of the door.
Feel free now,
there is no constrainment,
no need to hide
for lack of raiment.
A cotton sheet on the sofa
provides for good hygiene.
When it's cool in the winter,
keep a blanket on the scene.
Soon you'll both be worthless.
You'll revert to flowers in your hair.
Learn not to be reckless,
do not expose your derriere.
Keep a shade on the window
when you shed your shirt or blouse.
And be sure to keep the door shut
when you're naked in the house.

3-22-14

No Deer

I'm carrying a book in my back pocket,
tells me how to hunt like Davey Crockett.
In the woods early, under the moon,
I hunted through the hot afternoon.

One had his white tail up and nose in the air,
running Nascar fast away from here.
I'm gonna call Old Hiawatha, up on Lake Gitchee Gumee,
for help to make my hunts not end up so gloomy.

He might be a cow horn spike or a fork horn,
grazing all night on a row of sweet corn.
I've got a place for him in my crock-pot.
He's welcome to dinner, I just need one shot.

On the grill they smell so sweet,
but they take a while to peel and eat.
So what's a man like me to do
to get a pot of venison stew?

Are you sure Daniel Boone did it this way?
Sure costs a lot to get a deer these days.
On the highway up ahead;
a neon sign glows yellow and red.

'Cause down at the cafe "Twixt 'n Tween,"
it's chopped and mixed, and nice and lean.
It's barbeque tonight. Only pork, I fear;
tonight they feed a hungry man – with no deer.

12-2-13

Sharpshooters

I knew two men in my town,
they were adults when I was small.
I said I knew them, though not
very well, as I recall.

They lived the standard,
average lives back then,
did what was expected
of men like them.

Worked at the mill
and put up with their wives –
they paid the standard price required
to live their average, comfortable lives.

They dined Friday nights
at the local buffet,
attended church once a year,
every Easter Sunday.

Both had children at home
that brought them pain.
They hung over their dads' heads
just like clouds that spit rain.

Whether it was stress from home
or the daily job routine,
both men lost their zeal,
they both had forgotten dreams.

Each man, while looking
for an easy way out,
seemed to have forgotten
what life is all about.

They both had the same thought.
They would hasten their own end
by propping a shotgun up under their chin.
They would then pull the trigger and go out like men.

They really did this,
just a few weeks apart.
And I know you think
this should tug on the strings of your heart.

But the strange thing is, both of these guys missed.
While I'm sure they never tried it again,
all these great marksmen did
was blow off both of their chins.

The paramedics came
and rushed them away,
saved their mundane lives
just for practice, as they say.

Then two wise and learned surgeons
in a hospital downtown
worked hours building jawbones
that might grind their food enough to send it down.

They used a little plastic,
transplanted a little bone.
After weeks of "chewing therapy,"
they sent their patients home.

A funny thing about all those
man made parts,
surgeons will tell you right
from the start,

they're never as good
as the ones you had,
" 'cause God don't
make anything bad."

I had occasion to see
both men chew.
It was like watching
an animal at the zoo,

sort of like a camel
chewing on his cud,
or maybe a giraffe
high above all the mud.

It was quite a sight
if you cared to peek.
The mouths would gape open,
and their lips would leak.

Now I don't know for sure,
and I wouldn't swear,
but they say the bone that was used
came from their own derriere.

Now I never stopped to ponder
what this might mean,
but there's a bone from their own hineys
where their chins used to be.

Now when they look in the mirror,
as we all do now and then,
I wonder if they're reminded
who they see is a big rear end.

7-23-14

-§-
*Ending a sentence with a preposition is
something up with which I will not put.*
Winston Churchill

The Lazy Man

Why stand up straight
    when you can lean against the wall?
The Lazy Man, while thinking,
    considers it all.

    Why stand at all
        when you can sit?
    The way the Lazy Man
        looks at it.

        Why even sit
            when you can lay down?
        The Lazy Man reclines
            on whatever's around.

    Why use energy
        chewing tough beef?
    The Lazy Man always
        saves his teeth.

The Lazy Man has
    his meat finely ground.
Besides, ground beef
    is cheaper by the pound.

The Lazy Man listens
    to his own brain.
Why fix the roof
    if it leaks when it rains?

    He just sets a bucket
        on the floor.
    It won't bother him
        anymore.

        To take his thought
            to the "nth degree"
        is dangerous,
            it seems to me.

    If he becomes too lazy
        to draw his own breath,
    will he be satisfied
        with his own death?

To embalm this man
    would be a waste. Would it not?
This Lazy Man is too
    lazy to rot!

3-26-14

-§-

People who throw kisses are hopelessly lazy.
Bob Hope

Dentally Challenged

I went down home last week to see my kin.
It sure was good to see all of them again.

I saw a cousin of mine
I hadn't seen in years.
I noticed right off
most of his teeth had disappeared.
> When he shook my hand
> and began to smile,
> he looked like a
> snaggle-toothed crocodile.
>> I said, "Hey cuz, what happened
>> to your choppers?"
>> He said, "I got a set of lowers,
>> and I'm waitin' for my uppers."

He said, "All my teeth was healthy
'til I married ole Pearl.
Then I ran afoul of her mean
brother, Earl.
> "I lost my left incisor
> and a canine tooth that day.
> Well, it looked pretty bad,
> 'til the swellin' went away.
>> "I lost another incisor,
>> when I came home late one night.
>> I thought Pearl would be asleep –
>> wrong – we had a fight.

"I forgot Pearl thinks of her
brass knuckles as jewelry,
and that's the last time I go home
smellin' like a brewery."
    So I asked my kin if he and Pearl
    were still together.
    He said, "Shoot yeah, man,
    she's the best one for me, whatever.
        "She's great in the kitchen,
        she can really cook a meal,
        and I'll get to eat one soon,
        if my mouth would ever heal.

    "Me leave Pearl? Man, you're talkin' silly,
        I'd lose that free dental care
        I get from her little brother, Billy!"

Well, that's about all,
except Aunt Ider's cow had twins,
well sorta, only four hooves between them,
with a head on either end.
    But that can't compare with what
    happened here last weekend.
    Uncle Leroy's Holstein calf
    had no head, just two rear ends.
        Uncle Leroy said he really liked it
        better that way.
        It means more meat for him.
        You can't eat them horns anyway.

10-16-13

Wackos and Liars

Wackos and liars and walkers on wires
      should have no great place on this earth.
There's some consternation and deliberation
        over their value and worth.

The wackos I've seen fit somewhere between
      a squirrel always chewing a nut
and a boy or a girl in their own little world,
        who needs a swift kick in the butt.

Liars come along to knowingly wrong
      anyone who may be in their way.
And it's all self-promotion without any emotion,
        disregarding the ones left dismayed.

Those that walk wires are just like the liars,
      if it all doesn't go just as planned.
They come tumbling down, and both hit the ground,
        and leave a mess to clean up in the end.

7-7-13

The Bathtub

It's there when you need it,
this cast iron delight,
in the bleary-eyed morning
or dark of the night.

Or, when the toilet hangs out
a No Vacancy sign
when it's occupied
by another's behind.

The bathtub's so handy,
so easy to hit.
The wonder is, we don't
often think to use it.

It's shining so brightly
in the warm morning sun
for any man or boy anxious
to do "number one."

It's there when you need it,
an easy target in a rush.
But while it's easier to hit,
it's harder to flush.

2-16-14

Morning Banter*

One weekend morning
in their English home,
a women seeks to shower
and find some time alone.
    Her old man enters shortly
    to avail himself the loo.
    He hears water running
    and knows what he has to do.
He wants to raise her spirits
and make her laugh some too.
So even on the weekend,
daily "aggravation time" is due:
    He asks, "Are you washing your bum, mum?"
    No answer from the woman.
    "Did you rid it of scum, mum?"
    She says, "Go away old man," and laughs.
"If you need help, I'll arrange some."
She says, "No thank you," as she laughs.
"A wire brush should get it done, mum."
She sighs loudly, and laughs.
    "Have you been in the rum, mum?"
    "No, but," she says, "It's clear
    I'm gonna need some,
    if you're here all day with me!"
And so it goes with those two,
together over forty years.
Their love and sense of humor
keep their home fresh and free from tears.

1-4-14
*To be read in your worst English accent

At the Zoo

It fell our lot
June of this year,
to enlighten two children
we hold so dear,

both of them, each
a beloved grandchild,
to teach them about
the animals wild.

A fearsome task
for anyone to do.
But still, we took them
to the zoo.

The sun was hot;
still was the air.
Not a cloud in the sky,
no shadows anywhere.

The lion roared and complained
from atop his rock.
Submerged and cool
stayed the gator and the croc.

While the sun beat down
on the leafy trees,
I began to smell
like the chimpanzees.

Down the path and
around the lake,
a sign told us
about seats we could take

at a small arena
back in the pines,
to see a show that day
all about sea lions.

The sea lion came out
and looked around,
stole the trainer's fish,
and with a single bound,

jumped back into
his water so cool.
I could tell the sea lion
was nobody's fool.

And since it was in the hot summertime,
there was a pool where the children could play.
They were cool, at last,
by the end of the day.

While the lion roared
from atop his rock,
complaining of "heat rash"
around the clock,

the polar bears
all went on strike
and made a call to PETA
about the lack of ice.

The hyenas then laughed me
out of the zoo
for smelling worse
than a sweaty mule.

6-20-14

-§-

If you're hanging around with nothing to do and the zoo is closed, come over to the Senate. You'll get the same kind of feeling and you won't have to pay.
Bob Dole

Bank on It

My giant bank
    is so good to know.
They put my check from
    another bank on hold.

    For seven days
        it has to rest,
  while the interest it draws,
        will feather their nest.

Corporate America has my back.
    I've been told with a straight face,
money that's mine
    can't leave their place.

    It's for my own good,
        I politely was told,
  that the bank put all
        my money on hold.

Larger checks must
    clear the bank,
smiled the bubble-brained,
    bleach-blonde skank.

God forbid, I should
    try to spend
or pay a debt
    that's due to end.

I must toe the line
    like the other fools
who live their lives
    by bankers' rules.

Not much interest
    do I get,
to let them hold
    my money yet.

One more debt
    for me to pay,
and when that debt
    is swept away,

no more bankers
    will I stand.
I'll keep my money
    in a coffee can.

6-7-14

The Chicken

A chicken followed me home last night,
    not one with feathers and feet.
But one who was roasted on a stick,
    golden brown and ready to eat.

Followed me, in the loosest sense of the word.
    (It rode behind me in my Jeep).
It was still and polite
    there in the sack, it never made a peep.

But once upon the table,
    it began to communicate with me.
She convinced me she was held captive,
    and with one bite, she would be set free.

I tried so hard to ignore her
    and wait 'til my wife came home.
But the bird kept on insisting
    that she and I should dine alone.

Then suddenly it happened,
    she released her aroma from the box.
It was as if I were intoxicated.
    This chicken was some kind of fox!

With her tanned legs tucked
    there by her wings,
this chicken was truly
    a beautiful thing.

All that tender white meat
    put me to the test.
I took a fork
    and cut into her breast.

As I tasted the
    warm, moist meat,
I knew my crime
    was so incomplete.

I must continue to dine alone
    and consume this bird,
then hide the evidence
    before the wife gets word.

Too late! I heard her
    at the door.
She was gonna be mad
    and hungry, for sure.

I tried hard to explain
    with my face in my hands.
I said, "You don't know what a spell
    she can put on a man."

"Who is this she?" my wife demanded,
    and wanted to know.
"The bird, the bird!" I screamed, pointing
    at the pile of bones below.

She said, "I'm eating out,
    I'm ready to leave.
That appetite of yours
    is hard to believe."

I began to stare at
        what was left of the bird.
Her bones stared back
        without a word.

I asked, "Can we not commune,
        just you and me,
like when you asked me
        to set you free?

"Because now my wife is gone.
        I'm all alone,
and she didn't say
        what time she'd be home."

As I waited for the
        bird's reply,
I noticed something
        with my watery eyes.

The chicken made no
        remarks as before,
for on the table her bones were forming a word.
        Wrote the chicken, "Nevermore."

        Only this and nothing more.

7-9-14

Game Time

Poems

-§-
I would rather be in the arena to be excited or be disappointed than not have a chance at all. That's football. That's why everybody plays it.
Peyton Manning

The Game

It's with us still, even when we're old.
Once you taste it, your love for it won't ever grow cold.

It enters in as the sweat leaves the pores.
The brain and the heart, even the nose, are its doors.

It's hammered in deep, the late summer and fall,
with cuts and abrasions and bruises for all.

At some certain point, your body's had enough.
For your legs and joints, this game is too rough.

So you now buy a ticket or see the game on TV.
Whether playing or watching, this game ain't for free.

As you watch a slick tailback cut into the line,
and leave all the slow-footed defenders behind,

you can recall all the times in your yard that you played,
or remember your old high school glory days.

You've seemed to forgotten you old bruises and bumps,
'cause when your favorite team plays, your adrenaline pumps.

We cheer them, the young, and curse being old.
And we still love the game that seeps into our soul.

11-3-13

The Stadium

The stadium, the practice field, the yellow sun –

> I see them later in life on a September day
> in colors of yellow, green, and shadowed grey.
>
> > They're still familiar and sweet to me,
> > unlike many other memories.
>
> The school is gone now, like a lot of my friends.
> Looking back, we all held so much promise then.

The stadium, the practice field, the yellow sun –

> They still wait for me, call my name, and urge me on.
> They know it's one place where I still feel at home.
>
> > While they wait for me with little change,
> > I just grow older and show my age.

The stadium, the practice field, the yellow sun –

> affect me still, at my age, even to this day.
> It's where I gave so much of myself away.
>
> > It's where, with hard work and sweat,
> > you learn to earn every yard that you get.
>
> It's where every little bit of gain
> is purchased with fatigue and pain.

The stadium, the practice field, the yellow sun –

> One thing I loved about the stadium,
> no place in the world had such a golden yellow sun.
>
>> It was always yellow, never red,
>> etched forever on my heart, in my head.
>
> And now that I am growing old,
> it will be forever in my soul.
>
>> Each fall, I thank God for what was done.
>> I became a man whether
>> the game was lost or won.
>> At the stadium, the practice field,
>> and in that hot, yellow sun.

9-3-13

My Buddy Joe

In Heaven, when I've found
all the people that I love,
there'll be my buddy Joe
with a baseball and his glove.

He'll have to be there with me
to help me compete
on the real *Field of Dreams*,
that makes Heaven complete.

We played all the sports
we could in our youth.
Sometimes we got shut out,
just to tell you the truth.

But on every occasion,
we took our pound of flesh.
It's strange in life, how
some memories stay fresh.

Come Friday nights in our town,
just like them all,
we turned on the big lights,
then we played football.

I was a tackle,
my nose down in the line.
Joe was a safety,
just a few steps behind.

Joe may have been too light,
but he always did his part.
He was so much bigger
when you factored in his heart.

Sports had left us both with
a permanent limp.
He had a metal ankle,
and me, a metal hip.

But his great heart failed him,
and a few years have gone by.
He's on the All-Star Team in Heaven,
up in God's own sky.

Sometimes I remember how we
pushed each other then.
It had a strange way of turning
all of us boys into men.

But the next time I see him
with a football in his hands,
he'll holler, "Go long and catch
it, if you can!"

He'll throw a perfect spiral;
the ball will hit me in my hands.
Then I'm sure I'm gonna drop it,
just to hear him laugh again.

12-17-13

Our Team

So why does it always seem to you
your team is short a player or two?
> "We need one more right-handed pitcher.
> We don't have any southpaws, either.
> Our town's forever played baseball well.
> Now our teams really stink, they smell."

So look around, and it should be clear,
all those same genetics still are here:
> our Dads, with shoulders broad and strong,
> who once hit the ball so hard and long,
> Mom's wide hips to conceive and bring forth,
> have fewer kids than ever before.

But that is only half the reason
you're having such a losing season.
> The power hitter you've all desired,
> his birthday was completely denied.
> His mom and dad just wanted a girl,
> so he never made it to this world.

It's way too easy to sweep away
the boys who should be playing today.
> But that's the law, what can you do?
> Maybe recruit a player or two?
> And when it comes to football season,
> cheerleaders here, to the eyes, aren't pleasing.

If pretty mothers have pretty girls,
then there's the shortage in your world,
  'cause the pretty girls of your generation
  bought the same lie as all the nation.
  "It's best to stay so trim and skinny.
  So children? We aren't having any."

And if somehow they miscount their pills,
and then their wombs begin to fill,
  they always know
  just what to do,
  what clinic they
  should travel to.

But let's talk about our football team.
To win the big trophy is our dream.
  This year the defense is still intact,
  but good luck finding a quarterback.
  Find a quarterback by summer,
  or this season will be a bummer.

There's one player you would have had today.
His first trimester, he was flushed away.
  His dad played great
  here as quarterback.
  He might be the player
  that you lack.

So how do I know all this stuff you ask?
I saw his would-be mom just Sunday last.
  She spoke of living with guilt and shame,
  since she swept away his life, his name.
  She told me she'd had nothing but pain,
  and she hears him cry every time it rains.
  Now she hears his voice in the falling rain.

5-19-13

Baseball Time

Old winter is leaving.
      Spring's coming on fast.
All young boys know that
          when they smell the new grass.

    When you all run home from school,
         leave your jackets inside.
    Grab your bat, ball, and glove;
           a new season's arrived.

Be the first to show up
      at the old vacant lot.
Find stuff to use for bases,
        anything you've got.

    Some old shingles, cardboard,
        or a garbage can lid,
    or use a dried up cow patty,
          like we sometimes did.

The friends we play ball with
      are our best friends for life.
We think of them after
        we have kids and a wife,

    remembering them fondly,
        half a century past,
    while it's hard to remember
          when we saw them last.

While we all get excited
    when the ball meets the bat,
as good as it is, there's something
        better than that.

    The first time you feel
        the ball pop in your glove,
    you've been introduced
        to your own first True Love.

To field your position
    brings pride, when it's done,
and of baseball's five tools,
        it is the first one.

    You may need all five
        to be Hall of Fame,
    but if you have one or two,
        you can still play the game.

To field and hit, hit for power,
    to throw and to run,
use the tools you were given –
        Play Ball and Have Fun!

6-24-13

-§-
Baseball is ninety percent mental
and the other half is physical.
Yogi Bera

The Fighter

Why does he do it? Answer the bell?
The fighter who's cut and his eyes have both swelled.

It's been a mismatch, he's lost from the start.
He knows he's beaten, everywhere but his heart.

It keeps on pumping and urging him on,
while the rest of him wants to quit and go home.

Once more he's knocked down, and as he looks for his feet,
he says, "I'm okay—I can fight," to the old Referee.

He knows how to win, and it's more than a hunch,
this late in the fight, he has to land a big punch.

Sometimes it happens, like a story in a book –
this fighter's opponent dropped by a left hook.

It would be so much easier if life were that way.
You would know who you were fighting from day to day.

So many times our lives are like a fight,
you struggle to answer the bell every night.

I've seen people hurting in times such as these,
absorbing life's blows, going down to their knees.

From the loss of a job, to the loss of a child,
so many people just run away and hide.

But please, dear God, bless all the ones
who battle on, 'til their battle is won.

Something in their DNA says,
"We won't quit. Not us. Not today."

We thank you, Lord, for those fighters with heart,
who don't need to see the end from the start,

who plod along down their own muddy road,
no matter how heavy and tiresome their load.

They've learned that you can rise over the pain life gives,
and the scars that you carry are the proof that you lived.

8-26-13

The Last Fourth Quarter

I ran into a friend
at a store I was in.
    It had been years since we'd met anyplace.
        We shook hands and smiled,
      and all of the while,
I noticed the change in his face.
Once an athletic fellow,
his belly was now Jello,
    his football physique, long gone.
        I thought, this can't be my friend,
        it doesn't look like him,
    something here is so wrong.
I remembered the times
we would trot up the line
    to face other teams' angry young men.
        I saw that time had flown fast,
      we are now part of the past,
we'll never be in that good shape again.
When the time came to leave,
we both lied and agreed
    that we looked good for men of our age.
        But no matter our plea,
      no one lives life for free;
we get caught in time's turning page.
We've lived in life's big arena,
and the Great Referee says
    time's growing short in the game.
        Whether on God's team or the other,
      an enemy or a brother,
time runs out on us all, just the same.

7-23-13

Poems

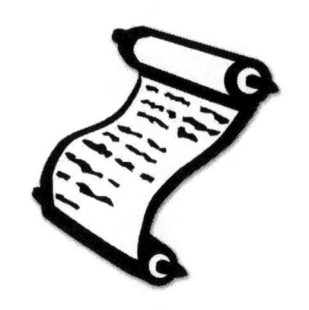

in General

Tread Gently

It read, "Tread Gently on the Earth,"
    there printed on an old T-shirt.
I asked myself, who would care
    how I move my feet, and where?

    The answer, then, came to me clear –
        the One who made the rocks and air.
    The world's a gift from God above,
        a special way to show His love.

For this old ground is more than dirt,
    it's where God came to heal our hurt,
since our lack of goodness was unearthed
    from Adam and Eve, the ground was cursed.

    It's where angel feet have trod
        to proclaim the Son of God.
    And where our only Savior tread,
        without a place to lay His head.

It's where He gave His life away
    to save us, who were made of clay.
Though He arose and left us here,
    His Holy Spirit's always near.

    God alone knows the time and date.
        For Christ's return, we'll have to wait.
    As for us, we'll bide our time
        on the rock where Christ did save mankind.

5-23-13

Heroes

Heroes are born on Earth everyday;
we never know when they'll come to be.
Here are some prime examples.
You may know someone like these.

Sean learned to shoot under watchful eyes.
He was raised by his old granddad.
He turned out to be one of the finest shots
the US Army ever had.

It was said he had nerves of steel,
and his blue eyes were always clear.
They said he had a lion's heart
and that he knew no fear.

A sniper's role he played in the war,
from Iraq to Afghanistan.
The effect a sniper has on the foe,
only a warrior can understand.

Lives were saved because of him.
Men now live who would have died.
A silver star was awarded him.
In battle he turned the tide.

Sara was small for her age when she started school,
and her adoptive parents were poor.
They scrimped and saved to educate her,
so her own mind could open up doors.

She studied hard in school,
excelled in science and math.
Scholarships were offered;
research became her chosen path.

Sara's work is her life,
as with many great minds.
When all the time, a cure for AIDS
is what she was hoping to find.

She is celebrated for what she's done.
Students study her work today.
Cures for diseases later were found,
because of the base she had laid.

Sean was a hero in the Middle East,
we all know that's true,
but there's another hero in his story,
don't let that escape you.

Sean's granddad took him in
when he was left all alone.
He swallowed his pride when his daughter
went wild, and raised Sean as his own.

Sean returned home as soon as he learned
his granddad passed away.
He traveled far, bringing the Silver Star
he'd earned, to place on his granddad's grave.

And Sara's work has touched us all
and all the world, far and near.
She might have lived her life in an orphan home.
Her folks adopted her from there.

They worked extra hours every week
to care for this little girl,
never knowing what they did out of love
would have such an effect on the world.

Heroes are born here on Earth,
on every turn of life's page.
They come in every color, shape, and size,
and it doesn't matter what age.

Heroic acts are performed all around,
as sure as the stars shine above.
Some require bravery, some require strength,
all are performed out of love.

There are more heroes here
than the obvious ones.
Such as the mothers who gave birth
to this daughter and son.

It took strength to bear them
and love to give them away.
God's will was accomplished
by what they did that day.

4-7-14

The Parting

I know I was a burden
all the time we two were as one.
It seems I was always in your way.
I know you're glad our time is done.

I guess you're feeling better now,
since I've left without a sound.
The whole thing ended badly for me,
and I won't be back around.

I hear it happens like that a lot,
but sometimes hard feelings can soften.
I wish it would have worked for us.
Do you think about me often?

I've talked to other folks
who say they were mistreated.
It seems they were a lot like me,
not wanted or even needed.

So you're surprised to hear from me,
I thought you wouldn't be anxious.
I don't really have a voice, you see,
I live within your conscience.

I'll be back from time to time.
You may feel like you're being haunted.
All I needed was a chance,
to be born was all I wanted.

You didn't need to stick around;
I would have made it okay.
I would have lived and breathed
the sweet clean air of many a sunny day.

Yeah, you'll hear my voice from time to time.
You will come to hate it as well.
While I never got to live,
your life will now be hell.

I'll leave you alone for now.
You must think I'm such a cynic,
but you're the one who walked away,
and left my blood on the floor of the clinic.

12-20-13

-§-
You shall not murder.
Exodus 20:13

The New Man

I went to work there when
I was nineteen years old.
I needed some money in my pocket
and some peace for my soul.

    My own place to live,
    to hide from the rain,
    a chance to recover
    from things that brought pain.

That rainy day when
I walked in that place,
the surprise was all mine.
I was the only white face.

    I looked around to see
    some men roll their eyes;
    I got a few dirty looks
    from some of the guys.

But by and large,
most of them were kind.
They told me I had just
"left my boyhood behind."

The work would be hard,
they said, dirty and rough.
"But a big boy like you can do
it, if you're tough enough."

I was strong and hard
from playing football.
But these guys were huge.
Next to them, I was small.

But I worked hard and
listened to them well.
By summer I was just one
of the boys, I could tell.

Late that summer,
amid all the heat,
a new man was hired
in off the street.

He was like most of us,
young, dumb, and poor.
You could tell as much
by the clothes he wore.

But he was different from me
and the rest of the men.
He had different hair;
he had different skin.

The older blacks called him, politely,
that "bright fellow,"
for his skin wasn't black, or
white, red or yellow.

His hair was dark red,
not curly, but wavy.
He had lots of freckles,
like pepper in your gravy.

He talked a lot. He would laugh
and joke with me or you.
I got to know him some
when he worked on our crew.

He was okay to be around;
at work, he did his share.
But many guys were puzzled
by his skin and by his hair.

I was questioned daily,
"What kind of man is he?"
And I would always answer,
"I don't know what he might be."

This was getting kind of old and
it was making me sort of ill,
'cause I was sure he was assembled
by the Good Lord's grace and will.

The next time I was queried anything
about the new man,
I said, "I don't know where he came from,
but he's like us all, he's just a human."

He moved away before the fall,
packed his clothes and took a ride,
left us here to do our work,
moved his kids and his young bride.

I thought of him not long ago.
There is a way now, for sure, they say,
to find out about a man's lineage,
but you have to steal his DNA.

If those nosey ones could have done this,
having been so bold,
upon stealing the secret of his appearance,
would they have delved even deeper into his soul?

For people who are "different,"
fitting in can take a while.
While nobody can change their skin,
our acceptance can make them smile.

7-7-14

The Slow Lane

I'm thinking lately,
as senility nears,
life in the slow lane
will strip all of your gears.

You might be thinking
that you're doing okay,
Botox and plastic keep
the wrinkles away.

Prescription pills keep
your head feeling fine,
but someday soon, you'll
see the end of the line.

Jesus is coming,
bringing His Judgement Day.
No matter what, you
just can't wish Him away.

So keep on smiling with
that Colgate grin.
Mistreat your neighbors.
Ignore all your friends.

Disown your children.
Man, your fun never ends.
You just get one life;
can't live it over again.

Guess what I'm saying is
now that you're old,
it's time to give a little
thought to your soul.

Lady Clairol can sure
cover your gray,
but only Jesus takes your
sins all away.

I'll leave that thought
with you, and I hope it sinks in,
'cause we may never see
each other again.

But if our talk has caused
a change in your plan,
it's probably time you had
a talk with THE MAN.

He is easily found
when you're down on your knees,
inside a church,
or out under the trees.

If you're through denying,
and are ready to live,
He loves us all,
and He's quick to forgive.

2-28-13

Accident of Birth

When you talk about the state of man,
it only is what it is.
But there are things that happened along the way
that made us turn out like we did.

Where we are now, and where we were born,
I think I know in my heart,
some were left at the starting line,
while others had a head start.

All men are equal, women too,
and all deserve our respect.
But early in life, it seemed to me,
some of our brothers suffered neglect.

Would you plant a tree, ask it to grow
without water and sunlight too?
Then how could you ask your child to prosper
without love and nurture from you?

Some folks are born
in the lap of luxury,
and I wish them all well.
Some are born to a life of drudgery.

They make do with low-paying, back-breaking jobs.
They live much closer to hell.
They toil away everyday of their lives,
and struggle to answer the bell.

Their time here, while just as dear,
is all spent
earning money for food
and rent.

While they're just as smart
and work just as hard
as the cross-town, trust-fund kids,
their future, it seems, was all in the cards,

the bad hand of cards they were dealt
on their first day on earth.
They'll spend their lives overcoming the reality
of their "accident of birth."

2-24-14

Classic Class Warfare

The "Intelligentsia" met behind the White House Walls,
    the "Best and the Brightest,"
    the smartest of all,

    to talk about cures for society's ills,
        and how to increase their
        own dollar bills.

The "Learned One" said, "I don't want to sound rash,
    but our problem here is
    white trailer park trash.

    If I had my way, I'd line them up by a wall,
        and our own military could
        finish them all."

The "Pencil-Necked Geek" said, "Wait, not so fast.
    I know a way we can
    kill them for cash,

    and throw in latinos and blacks,
        with the trailer
        park trash."

The "Spin Doctor" said, "We'll make it sound so cool.
    They'll stand in a line and break
    God's strictest rule,

    'Women's Choice' clinics are long overdue."

The "Fat Cat from Wall Street," a banker I guess,
    said, "I see here a new
    place to invest.

    We'll make so much money when this plan evolves,
        and we'll see all of society's
        problems solved."

And so it has gone on for years and years.
    Babies have died, and yes,
    their mothers shed tears.

    And once again in this "great" nation of ours,
        the Poor and the Helpless are
        defeated and scarred.

So if you're thinking of making the choice,
    let your own child be born,
    so he can have his own voice.

    Never be so quick to assume
        that you owe nothing to the
        child in your womb.

8-1-13

-§-

*I've noticed that everyone who is for
abortion has already been born.*

Ronald Reagan

Unseen Hands

How long must you search
        'til you find your own voice?
The hands of life can stifle
        and leave you without choice.

They will grab you by your belt
        and spin you around,
just when you thought
        you were gaining ground.

The hand that continually
        and forcefully covers your throat
prevents your thoughts and words
        from rising high enough to float.

The hand that covers
        your lips and teeth
has a way to prevent you
        from being unique.

The hands can be felt
        but they're always unseen.
The hands of life
        can be downright mean.

It takes strength and will
        to be your own man,
to fight the pressure
        of the unseen hand.

To know when to be cautious
        and to know when to dare,
foretells a time yet to come
        when you make those
                hands disappear.

Learn to pick your battles
        on your own battlefield.
The more times you win,
        the better will be your skills.

It always costs to
        be your own man,
but the payoff comes
        if you never give in.

Then while you struggle
        with life's stern demands,
you can ask God above
        to lend you His two hands.

1-3-14

Vines

I don't drink whiskey and I stay away from bars.
The worst thing you can do is to drink and drive cars.
I did taste something that nearly blew my mind.
I tasted my friend Woody's muscadine wine.

He said, "I don't make much, just a little for myself.
You won't find nothing like it for sale on the shelf."
He said, "These vines grow fast and this place is so viney,
if you don't keep moving, they'll wrap around your hiney.

"But the Lord did good when He gave us all these vines,
'cause a whole bunch of them are full of muscadines.
You can make jelly with them and spread it on your bread,
or keep drinking my wine 'til it messes up your head.

"Either way you take it, it all tastes fine,
ain't nothing like the fruit of a muscadine vine."
That's my friend Woody—he ain't ashamed
to speak up and praise the Lord by name.

One more thing Woody said is true,
"Ain't nothing in this world the Lord can't do."

7-26-13

-§-
*Age is a question of mind over matter.
If you don't mind, it doesn't matter.*
Leroy "Satchel" Paige

One Hundred Four and Counting

Just doing my job
out in the heat,
utility work,
walking down the street.

On a hot July morning,
in the sun, near noon day,
I spoke to three black men
on their porch in the shade.

> "How old do you think he is?"
> one asked, pointing at the one nearest me.
> I said, "I would guess
> he's about sixty-three."

"He's one hundred and four.
We're his sons. He's our father.
We're keeping him out of the sun,
under orders from his daughter."

> I spoke up and told him how good he
> looked for a man of his age.
> He told me, "God's been good, but my
> daughter's trying to keep me in a cage."

> She had caught him red-handed
> before he was done
> toting buckets of water
> out in the sun

to give to his dogs
down on the back lot.
Half the way there
was as far as he got.

He said, "I don't understand
what's wrong with my daughter.
I was trying to give my dogs
a cool drink of water."

> He wore old gray pants
> and a plaid shirt.
> You could tell from his arms,
> he was used to hard work.

> Still straight and tall,
> he wanted to move around,
> not content to sit
> and let his body run down.

>> I said, "You've seen some changes
>> since you've been around."
>> He said, "I have. Life is much
>> easier now."

>> As I stood in the sun
>> and wiped sweat from my face,
>> I couldn't help but think,
>> this is a gift from God's grace.

One hundred and four years old,
still has his mind and use of his limbs.
His children still love him.
I was envious of him.

6-2-14

Questions

What does a man do with his restless soul
to quiet it down 'til he is old?
Too old for his legs to carry his mind for a ride,
over the next hill, just to see the other side.

Too old to investigate the *whats* and the *whys*
that make women weep and their babies cry.
We are never content with the *when* or the *where*,
but *why* is the answer we all seek to hear.

It's hard wired in us, born in the brain,
like the steady rumble of a slow moving train.
Questions need answers; some answers give pause.
Especially for us who've been told "just because."

When all of our running has left us quite lame,
and all of our cunning has left us in shame,
we'll still be in doubt about the *why* and the *how*,
and too shallow to care about much more than the *now*.

12-16-13

At the Indigo

Seven o'clock at the Indigo,
we'll have our meal and stay 'til time to go.

> We'll meet our friends there and talk and laugh,
> because we all came with our better half!

Wear your nice clothes, but they don't require a tie.
If I said I wasn't glad, it would be a lie.

> The food is good, but when the meal ends,
> we still have time to spend with our friends.

Friends in life are sometimes hard to find.
They are relationships that have been refined.

> In every friendship, there's a common thread,
> one that links each other's heart and head.

And if that thread can touch your soul and mine,
we'll have a friendship of the finest kind.

> For our friends, we thank the Lord above.
> We're bound together by His perfect Love.

9-26-13

Two Go In

I saw two go in; only one came out.
I began to ask, "What's that about?"

    I continued to see
    and now can confirm,
    two people went in,
    and only one returned.

    I asked someone,
    "What kind of place is this?"
    They didn't answer.
    I thought, "Something's amiss!"

    I saw women go in.
    Some came out in tears.
    I found out this has
    gone on for years.

    We're all concerned
    about saving the whales.
    Hurt one of them
    and you go to jail.

I'm for saving the forest
and the spotted owl, so wild,
but I'm really worried
about the Human Child.

How long can we go on
with our heads in the sand
and still not preserve
the Children of Man?

Two humans go in;
only one comes out.
It should make us mad,
there is no doubt.

How can they say
this practice is safe?
When, if we all did this, it's
"Goodbye, Human Race!"

This is the only medical
practice, I would guess,
that kills half of its patients
and remains a success.

I think I know now how this game is played.
"If a baby don't die, nobody gets paid."

6-12-14

Rooms of Our Hearts

Do we know today why we seem so afraid
of making new friends like the ones that we've made?
    Why in the world do we still push away
        those who could sweeten our lives every day?

Is it the color of skin, or texture of hair,
or their style of clothes, or tattoos that they wear?
    Not any of these can keep us apart,
        but what resides in the rooms of our hearts.

Our mind takes a seat to let jealousy rage,
and remains on his rear while hate takes the stage.
    Greed is act three; he plays his part so well.
        And lust has a room in our heart where he dwells.

But let's watch, if you will, the face of a young child.
When he meets a new person, he lights up and smiles.
    Our kids don't have all the marks of a hater.
        When taught to by us, it all shows up later.

We think it's odd and don't comprehend
why they don't think like women and men.
    The answer's from above, and don't think it's so odd.
        Christ said, "Such as these are the kingdom of God."

6-21-13

A Need for Speed

There's somebody who's
been coming around.
He wants to see you
six feet in the ground.

> He's in your mind
> for no good reason,
> a voice for which
> there is no pleasing.

>> "You're no good,
>> can't do anything right."
>> He wakes you up,
>> even late at night.

But you can't hear him at all
when you're on your bike.
The sweet roar of the engine
makes everything right.

> You're hearing the devil;
> he's creating a need;
> he's instilling in you
> a love for speed.

>> You hear the roar
>> when you hit the starter.
>> You lean into the wind
>> and drive it harder.

Out on the freeway
late one night,
not another soul
is in sight.

>Your tires are warm.
>The asphalt's level.
>That's when you get
>the last word from the devil.

>>"Open this bike up,
>>be wild and free;
>>ain't nothing in the world
>>like running with me!"

With him in your head
and your hand on the throttle,
you're driving reckless,
like you've been on the bottle.

>When you crash this bike
>and leave the road,
>he'll watch your head
>to see how far it will roll.

>>When they scrape you up
>>and fill that body bag,
>>it's a scene that can make
>>a strong man gag.

So the devil wins
another round;
he's taken another
good man down.

    He's left your family
    a heavy load.
    He just laughs and says,
    "One more for the road."

        Satan doesn't tempt with
        just money and fame.
        He'll use anything to send
        your soul to flames.

He'll use drugs and sex
and sports or whiskey;
under his guidance
anything's risky.

    So keep a watch,
    and you might try praying.
    And listen to what the
    Bible is saying.

        Then ask the Lord,
        "Is this good for my soul,
        or will it take me
        where I don't want to go?"

1-10-13

Federalies

Somewhere down the line
it all slipped away,
at the notion of being polite.
Please, let me speak of it, if I may.

From the results of that day,
all men I know pay the price.
We now bite our tongues 'til they are numb
to suppress words thought not to be nice.

I'm not saying, "Let's curse
to add bite to our verse."
That does strain society's bounds.
But to filter each word leaves free speech unheard.

If I can't speak
my mind aloud,
no matter who or what is around,
the whole idea is unsound.

To be so
politically correct,
it's someone's ears
we protect

'til we can't exercise
our own mouth.
Now we see
our nation's gone south.

It now seems
you and I
may be watched,
as if we are spies.

If our government
has its way,
our freedom may end
on not what we do, but what we say.

While the NSA reads our mail
and the FBI taps our phones,
we'll be running from jail
and hiding from drones.

From now on
it might be a sin
to let unfiltered words
go out or come in.

There shall be
no loose talk.
And at bad jokes
you should balk.

The whispers and laughter
shall cease,
lest with tongue and/or pen
women and/or men
OFFEND THE EAR OF THE FEDERAL POLICE.

1-17-14

For Noah

They took his name straight from the Bible,
and then he took his grandma's heart.
If love's a crime, then she was liable.
No one could keep the two apart.

Hers was the big house by the highway;
his was the smaller one behind.
It was so easy for him to visit,
his mom and dad would never mind.

Theirs was a bond that would grow stronger;
they grew closer as long as she would live.
But she couldn't stay here any longer;
she took all the hurt that life could give.

Now she has a house on Heaven's Highway,
with a smaller one behind.
And in the far-off future someday,
we know just what she has in mind.

A special place where they can visit,
a Christmas tree for Noah in every room.
She'll be the first one he will greet
in heaven, high above the moon.

His Grammy is gonna be there waiting.
One more thing to keep in mind –
God's Heaven's gonna last forever;
it's where they won't run out of time.

7-7-13

-§-
*I am reminded of your sincere faith,
a faith that dwelt first in your grandmother Lois
and your mother Eunice and now,
I am sure, dwells in you as well.*
2 Timothy 1:5

Tattooed

A tattooed man
sat among us.
Did a five year old artist
use his arms for a canvas?

They were colored in red,
blue, and green, and yellow;
spider webs were drawn
around each elbow.

My wife and I gazed
in wide-eyed wonder.
What kind of spell
was this guy under?

Alcohol or
something stronger?
His natural skin will be
seen no longer.

A new way to look stupid?
This guy has found it.
And it's hard to wrap
my head around it.

You see, I don't need
tattoos of moons and stars,
'cause on my body
I carry scars

from fistfights
in my other life,
from hospital stays
with a surgeon's knife,

from dog bites (even
one from a wolf),
from football games
back in my youth.

Tattoos used to
stand for something,
worn by soldiers, sailors,
or Marines.

Now they're worn by
those in this land
to extol the virtues
of Spiderman.

11-1-13

The Hound

A puppy I raised from the day he was born
continues to bite me,
    so be forewarned.

    He will no longer attack with his teeth;
    from his assaults,
        I need some relief.

The love I gave him seems to be forgotten.
His attitude toward me has turned
    from good to rotten.

    I paid for his training and medical bills,
    but now this dog seems
        to bear me ill will.

I dried him off when he was wet,
kept him warm in the winter,
    and will do so yet.

    I paid for his food, fed him off of my own plate.
    Now I feel teeth that bite
        and see eyes that hate.

Though he comes 'round and wags his tail
in front of everyone,
    it's me who gets nailed.

Should I repay this ungrateful hound
and keep his feet away from my
    own house and grounds,

or waste my time returning evil with good,
or beat him severely, like
    I one time would?

Maybe he should just stay away.
Another hound can be had
    at a good price today.

But I know the woman here loves him so,
and it would hurt her
    to let him go.

So at some time when she is not around,
I'll have my talk with
    this young hound.

Fur may fly and blood may spill,
but I'll prove my point,
    I swear I will.

For no one man, or dog, or mouse,
will disrespect me
    in my own house.

9-3-14

Home

Home – most of us have one.
Lots of us do not.
A place to keep you warm and dry,
or cool off when it's hot.

It can be a mansion on a hill,
or an apartment in the city,
a shotgun house on a ghetto street
with a view that's not so pretty.

Every home should be, for
every child, his own welcome place.
Is it too much to ask of you adults
to put a smile upon your face?

I know what it does to little ones,
parents constant criticism.
You mold them by what you do and say,
so you need to use some wisdom.

If he lives in a place where he's not loved,
or maybe not even wanted,
the effect of your words and deeds,
or lack thereof, means his life forever haunted.

When God in Heaven made us all,
He caused each child to love each parent.
They come here new, with His rule; that's true,
though there's no reason apparent.

I know you think your boy's so bad,
but there's no need to beat and shake him.
He needs a dad to help him along,
not one to abuse then forsake him.

Yeah, he'll always remember his own dad,
but he'll go on with the business of living.
And one day when you're old, you will
wish to your soul that you had been forgiven.

11-17-13

The Innocents Lost

There are laws in this world
written on the heart of man:
common sense to all,
what you can't do, what you can.

> They protect the rich and poor,
> the strong and weak.
> They also protect
> the mild and the meek.

Civilization in
its purest form
never veers very far
from this natural norm.

> We don't rob or steal,
> plunder or pillage,
> like pirates of old
> raiding a seaside village.

Our laws protect everything
in the world you can name,
except the innocent ones,
who can shoulder no blame.

> You can't rob from me,
> nor I from you,
> but you can steal the life of a child
> before his due date comes true.

We can't violate
anyone's civil rights,
but if they're still in the womb,
we say it's alright.

> We can prosecute
> with extreme prejudice
> any child unborn,
> as if they don't exist.

Would somebody please
tell me again
why it's one second after birth
we become a citizen?

> You've heard it before,
> let me lay it out plain,
> on the inside or out,
> that child is still the same.

There is a crime
being committed here
against the innocent ones,
who should be held so dear.

> One day soon, even now,
> we will see the cost
> of not protecting
> those innocents lost.

1-23-14

Whisper

Seems we all get in trouble
for what we say;
if it ain't happened yet,
it's coming your way.
>For those of us
>who don't understand,
>a mouth that works
>is what makes you a man.

Do you stay in line
with the status quo,
not ever revealing
the truths you know?
>Is it shame you feel,
>or is it fear,
>that keeps your mouth, your mind
>and brain out of gear?

There will be a time soon,
in this sweet land,
when we won't be allowed
to speak like a man.
>So say what you mean
>and mean what you say.
>Prepare your mind
>for that ominous day

when it will be time
to whisper your innermost thoughts
only to those ears you can trust,
not to those ears who've been bought.

9-15-14

The Critical Man

I wonder if he thought he
should act that way.
He was on his son's back
every minute, every day.

He hated the way his son
combed his hair;
he hated the clothes
his son chose to wear.

He never gave him
one minute of peace
and his criticisms
never seemed to cease.

He was always ready
to grab him and shake him,
but never worried
about what might break him.

When he was fifteen years old,
and big and strong,
the boy said, "This has gone on
for way too long."

So he challenged the man
for his own right just to breathe.
And for a while,
his dad let him be.

The mom sometimes
tried to take her son's part,
but the dad had bullying
down to an art.

Many years later
she apologized.
"He was just high strung,"
she had surmised.

"That old man was just mean,"
was the son's reply,
"And you know that
as well as I."

She just hung her head
and looked away;
nothing else has been said of it,
even to this day.

Neighbors and kin
apologized to the youth.
They weren't fooled by the dad,
they knew the truth.

But the boy is a man now,
with kids of his own.
He tried never to hurt
his family, now grown.

He never understood
what makes a man
injure his loved ones
with his words or his hands.

Could it be that a man
who, to a child, seemed so strong,
had a hole in his heart
where love should belong?

Whatever the problem,
I hope my dad got it straight
and made his peace with God,
before it was too late.

12-26-13

Green

I've thought about it,
and to tell you the truth,
green must be the
color of youth.

  A fresh recruit is always
  said to be green.
  That's never said
  about the old or in between.

When fruit is too young,
we can see it's green.
Later on when it ages,
it has a different sheen.

  It's the color of leaves
  that provide summer shade,
  a place to relax
  when your workday is "made."

You can be green with envy,
or have those jealous green eyes;
to have these emotions
just shows you're alive.

Green is the grass
where children like to play.
Green grass grows between
the red infield clay.

Green grass stays with us
on into the fall,
on the stadium floor,
where the young men play ball.

It stains your pants and jerseys,
affects the bounce and the roll.
You'll remember it's smell
wherever you go.

Green trees of Christmas
are part of our youth,
where Christ's birth is retold
and still rings with His truth.

6-26-14

-§-
*Whoever trusts in his riches will fall,
but the righteous will flourish like a green leaf.*
Proverbs 11:28

The Patch

There is a sorrow,
there is a guilt,
two patches on the
same patchwork quilt.

When the quilt is sewn,
it hangs in a frame.
Adding sorrow and guilt
would bring it shame.

Sorrow washes clean,
it just needs time,
but guilt will stain your
soul, your mind.

Another patch
would be the cure:
Forgiveness –
the patch that will endure.

11-4-13

-§-
A good book has no ending.
Robert Frost

Acknowledgments

First, let me thank my good friend and Pastor, Jason Dollar, for all the encouragement and help he has given me since I began this journey. An author himself he does all the brainwork (that I'm not equipped to do) required to publish a book.

Secondly, my appreciation goes to my good friend, Liz Roberts, who typed my stuff, then stored it in some dark part of her computer, and is the master of something called spellchecker. She also introduced me to the joys of whiteout. Thank you, Elizabeth. I promise to learn to type.

Next, I am grateful for my editor, Sandra Muir, whose compassion for this clown with a pen in his hand is exceeded only by her worth as a friend and sister in Christ. She is a part of our church, Rock Mountain Lakes Baptist Church, a family of faith that has encouraged me greatly in this project.

Lastly, I thank my family for being an endless supply of inspiration for these poems. And especially my sweet wife, Peggy, for taking a chance on a boy who was your total opposite, and making him "almost fit for church," at times anyway. Also, thanks for the great job you do with our family. You are the best ever.

If you have comments or questions for the author,
please send an email to nearstraightrows@gmail.com.

Made in the USA
Columbia, SC
19 February 2025